Henry Kiddle

Brown's language lessons with graded exercises in analysis

Henry Kiddle
Brown's language lessons with graded exercises in analysis
ISBN/EAN: 9783743417359

Manufactured in Europe, USA, Canada, Australia, Japa

Cover: Foto ©Paul-Georg Meister /pixelio.de

Manufactured and distributed by brebook publishing software (www.brebook.com)

Henry Kiddle

Brown's language lessons with graded exercises in analysis

BROWN'S
LANGUAGE LESSONS

WITH

GRADED EXERCISES

IN

ANALYSIS, PARSING, CONSTRUCTION, AND COMPOSITION

AN INTRODUCTION

TO

GOOLD BROWN'S SERIES OF ENGLISH GRAMMARS

BY

HENRY KIDDLE, A.M.

Late Superintendent of Schools, New York City

NEW YORK
WILLIAM WOOD AND COMPANY
1889

TROW'S
PRINTING AND BOOKBINDING COMPANY,
NEW YORK.

PREFACE.

The publication of this little manual is due to a demand, on the part of teachers who use Goold Brown's admirable system of English grammar, for an introductory work simpler and more elementary than the "First Lines," and supplied with more copious written exercises, and a system of diagrams for the illustration of sentential analysis.

In compliance with this demand, the book has been divided into easy lessons, and the *development system* has been more fully carried out in the presentation and elucidation of the whole subject. The work has, in this manner, been divested of the character of a formal treatise while the logical order of the topics has been still preserved. Nor is it a mere epitome of Brown's larger work, "The Institutes of English Grammar," but is to be regarded as a series of simple *Language Lessons*, involving the rudimentary principles, definitions, and rules of English Grammar, with abundant practice in their use and application, by means of both oral and written exercises, thus forming an introduction to the study of the larger work.

In all the lessons, the aim has been to divest the subject of the arbitrary and abstract character which has too often been given to grammatical study, and of which much complaint has justly been made. This has been avoided by developing in the mind of the pupil, by means of an easy and almost obvious analysis of simple examples, the ideas and distinctions designed to be imparted, after which formal definitions may properly be given. Thus every lesson, with its illustrative exercises in analysis and construction, becomes a step in training the pupil in the science and art of verbal expression, or language, and in leading him to the acquisition of correct habits in both speaking and writing. This is at present a very great *desideratum* in elementary education, not to be attained, as some think, by the abolition of what they are pleased to call "technical grammar," and the substitution of an arbitrary, hap-hazard method of practice, with no guide, principle, or rule, but by initiating the pupil into the knowledge and constant application of principles and rules, appealing at every step to his intelligence, and thus affording him that development of mind of which the rational study of grammar is so effective an instrument.

The system of diagrams employed in this work is designed to present clearly and forcibly, through the eye, the component parts of the sentence and their relations to each other, every relation being distinctly indicated by a special sign. This system has the advantage of complete perspicuity, so that the pupil, easily recognizing the relations indicated, may read the sentence as readily from the diagram as in its ordinary form. Hence, it will be found devoid of that complexity which, in most cases, has so greatly detracted from the value of this method of illustration, the diagram being often made more difficult to understand than the sentence which it is intended to explain. This method of graphically presenting the analysis of sentences, as soon as it has become familiar to the pupil, invariably becomes extremely fascinating to him, and serves to impress upon his mind those distinctions without a knowledge of which language can never be to the mind a definite means of expression, nor can ever be used with entire accuracy and clearness.

In the principles, rules, and definitions, the system of Goold Brown has been followed, with a very slight departure, for the sake of simplicity; and it is believed that, by this publication, that author's time-honored work may be rendered more valuable and more satisfactory to teachers and the general public.

NEW YORK, September 1, 1889.

CONTENTS.

LESSON	PAGE
I.—Language,	7
II.—Letters,	8
III.—Vowels and Consonants,	9
IV.—Elementary Sounds,	10
V.— " " Continued,	11
VI.—Consonant Sounds;	12
VII.—Syllables, Diphthongs, and Triphthongs,	14
VIII.—Diphthongal Sounds,	15
IX.—Syllables and Words,	17
X.—Division of Words into Syllables,	18
XI.—Simple and Compound Words,	19
XII.—Primitive and Derivative Words,	20
XIII.—Spelling,	21
XIV.—Spelling of Derivatives,	22
XV.— " " Continued,	23
XVI.—**Synopsis for Topical Review,**	25
XVII.—Names,	26
XVIII.—Subject and Predicate,	27
XIX.—The Sentence,	28
XX.—The Noun and the Pronoun,	29
XXI.—The Verb,	30
XXII.—The Article,	32
XXIII.—The Adjective,	33
XXIV.—The Adverb,	34
XXV.—The Conjunction,	35
XXVI.—The Preposition,	37
XXVII.—The Interjection,	38
XXVIII.—The Participle,	39
XXIX.—The Parts of Speech.—Review,	40
XXX.—Analysis of Sentences,	42
XXXI.—Analysis by Diagram,	44

LESSON	PAGE
XXXII.—Declarative and Interrogative Sentences,	45
XXXIII.—Imperative Sentences,	46
XXXIV.—Exclamatory Sentences,	47
XXXV.—Oral Analysis and Parsing,	48
XXXVI.—The Attribute,	50
XXXVII.—Compound Subjects and Predicates,	52
XXXVIII.—Phrases,	53
XXXIX.—Nouns and their Classes,	56
XL.—Modifications of Nouns.—Persons,	57
XLI.—Modifications of Nouns.—Numbers,	58
XLII.—Modifications of Nouns.—Genders,	59
XLIII.—Modifications of Nouns.—Cases,	61
XLIV.—Construction and Composition,	64
XLV.—Composition,	65
XLVI.—Classes of Adjectives,	66
XLVII.—Comparison of Adjectives,	69
XLVIII.—Simple and Compound Sentences,	71
XLIX.—Classes of Pronouns,	73
L.—Different Forms of Pronouns,	75
LI.—Compound Personal Pronouns,	77
LII.—Different Kinds of Adjuncts,	78
LIII.—Adverbial Adjuncts,	81
LIV.—Complex Sentences,	82
LV.—Construction.—Review,	84
LVI.—Construction, *Continued*,	85
LVII.—Compound Relative Pronouns,	86

CONTENTS.

LESSON	PAGE
LVIII.—Different Kinds of Verbs,	88
LIX.—Modifications of Verbs.—Moods,	89
LX.—Definitions of the Moods.—Review,	91
LXI.—Forms of the Moods,	92
LXII.—Tenses,	94
LXIII.—Forms of the Tenses,	95
LXIV.—Tense forms of the Verb "Be,"	97
LXV.—Participles,	98
LXVI.—Regular and Irregular Verbs,	99
LXVII.—Person and Number of Verbs,	101
LXVIII.—Conjugation of Verbs,	102
LXIX.—Compound Conjugations,	105
LXX.—Auxiliary and Defective Verbs,	106
LXXI.—Use of *Would* and *Should*,	107
LXXII.—Adverbs.—Classes,	109
LXXIII.—Conjunctions,	110
LXXIV.—Prepositions,	112
LXXV.—Use of Prepositions,	113
LXXVI.—Participial Phrases,	115
LXXVII.—Use of the Infinitive Mood,	117
LXXVIII.—Infinitive Object Clause,	119
LXXIX.—Compound and Complex Phrases,	120
LXXX.—**Synopsis for Topical Review,**	123
LXXXI.—Relation of Words,	124
LXXXII.—Agreement of Words,	126
LXXXIII.—Agreement.—Verbs and Subjects,	129
LXXXIV.—Agreement.—Connected Verbs,	130
LXXXV.—Agreement.—Subject and Attribute,	131
LXXXVI.—Agreement.—Pronoun and Antecedent,	132
LXXXVII.—Agreement.—Connected Antecedents,	134
LXXXVIII.—Government,	135
LXXXIX.—Government.—Prepositions,	137
XC.—Definitions.—Review,	138
XCI.—Different Kinds of Clauses,	139
XCII.—Subject and Attribute Clauses,	141
XCIII.—Object Clauses,	142
XCIV.—Infinitive Object Clauses,	143
XCV.—Adjective Clauses,	145
XCVI.—Adverbial Clauses,	146
XCVII.—Explanatory Clauses,	147
XCVIII.—Independent Clauses and Phrases,	148
XCIX.—Compound Sentences,	150
C.—**Synopsis for Topical Review,**	151
CI.—Use of Capitals,	153
CII.—Punctuation.—Review,	154
CIII.—Exercises in Construction,	156
CIV.—Composition.—Connection of Sentences,	157
CV.—Descriptive Compositions,	159
CVI.—Letter-Writing,	160
CVII.— " Forms of Address,	162
CVIII.— " Body and Closing,	163

APPENDIX.

List of Irregular Verbs,	165
List of Redundant Verbs,	169

LESSON I.

LANGUAGE.

For what purpose do people speak or write?
People speak or write to express their thoughts or feelings.

What do they use in speaking and writing?
They use words.

What is this mode of expressing thoughts or feelings called?
It is called **language**.

The word *language* is derived from the Latin *lingua*, the tongue.

What, then, is language?
Language is the expression of thought in speaking or writing.

Do all people use the same language?
No; people living in different countries generally use different languages.

Can you give some examples?
What language do we use in this country?
We use the English language.

How many ways of using language are there?
There are two ways of using language,—by speaking and by writing.

How many kinds of language, then, are there?
There are two kinds,—spoken language, or speech, and written language.

What are the simplest elements of language?
In spoken language, sounds; and in written language, letters representing those sounds.

To know how to use a language correctly, we must study its *grammar*.

English Grammar is the art of speaking and writing the English language correctly.

LESSON II.

LETTERS.

The teacher begins this lesson by writing on the blackboard several letters, and then proceeds :—

What are these marks, or characters?
They are letters.

What sounds do these letters denote?
[The pupils are to give the phonic elements.]
What are the names of these letters?

What must be learned in regard to each letter?
The *form* of the letter, its *name*, and the *sound* which it represents.

What is a letter?
A **letter** is a character used in printing or writing to represent a sound of the human voice.

The sounds of letters are sometimes called their *powers*.

The **alphabet** contains the names or forms of all the letters arranged in a certain order.

The letters used in English have two different forms. Thus :—

  A, B, C, D, E, F, etc.
  a, b, c, d, e, f, etc.

The larger letters are called CAPITALS ; the others, small letters.

Letters of this form are called Roman letters, because they were anciently used by the Romans.

There are, also, *Italic letters*, so called because they are the same as those used in the Italian language.

The form used in writing is called *script*. Thus :—

John is a good boy.

LESSON III.

VOWELS AND CONSONANTS.

How many letters are there in the English alphabet?
There are twenty-six.

Give their names in regular order.
Now try to give the sound of each.

Which of the letters have names the same as their sounds?
The letters **a, e, i, o, u.**

How are the names of the others formed?
Eight of them are formed by using the sound of the letter before *e*. These names are *be, ce, de, ge, pe, te, ve,* and *ze.*

Six are formed by using the sound of the letter after *e*. These are *ef, el, em, en, es,* and *ex.*

The others are variously formed; namely, *ja, ka, qu, ar, aitch, double-u,* and *wi.*

Which of the letters have complete sounds when they are uttered alone?
The letters a, e, i, o, and u.

These letters are called **vowels.**

The other letters of the alphabet are called **consonants.**

Why are they so called?
Because they must be joined to a vowel to be fully and clearly uttered.

_{The word *consonant* means *sounding with.*}

A **vowel** is a letter which forms a perfect sound when uttered alone.

A **consonant** is a letter which cannot be perfectly uttered till joined to a vowel.

Review.

What is language? Of how many kinds? What are the elements of language? What is a letter? What is the use of letters? What is the alphabet? Different forms of letters? What is a vowel? What is a consonant? What are the names of the vowels? How are the names of the consonants formed? What does the word *consonant* mean?

LESSON IV.

ELEMENTARY SOUNDS.

The elementary sounds, or powers of the letters, are either **vowel sounds** or **consonant sounds.**

Be careful to keep in mind the difference between the *letters* and their *powers*, or the sounds which they represent.

The elementary sounds are more numerous than the letters of the alphabet.

On this account some letters represent more than one sound, and some sounds are represented by combinations of letters.

For examples see the different sounds of the vowels below.

The **vowel sounds** are represented by the vowels or their combinations; as, *a* in *fall, fare, fat; ai* in *aim*, and *ou* in *out.*

The vowels represent different sounds in different words. The following are the sounds of *a:*—

The marks used with the letters, to distinguish the sounds, are called *diacritical marks*. The diacritical marks used are those of Webster's Dictionary.

ā (as in age), â (care), ä (art), ạ (all), ă (at), ȧ (ask), ạ (what).

ELEMENTARY SOUNDS.

The sounds of *e* are :—
ē (eve), e̱ (they), ê (there), ẽ (term), ĕ (end).

The sounds of *i* are :—
ī (ice), ĭ (pique), î (firm), ĭ (it).

The sounds of *o* are :—
ō (old), o̱ (do), ó (love), o̧ (wolf), ô (nor), ŏ (not).

The sounds of *u* are :—
ū (tune), u̱ (rude), û (urn), ṳ (pull), ŭ (but).

It should be observed that several of these letters with their marks represent the same sounds. Thus ā and e̱ are the same, and â and ê, also o̧ and ṳ; with some others.

The pupils should be thoroughly drilled in the enunciation of these elementary sounds.

LESSON V.

ELEMENTARY SOUNDS.—*Continued.*

Besides the vowels already named, the letter *y* is used as a vowel in some words. Its sounds are ȳ (try), ŷ (myrrh), y̆ (hymn).

It thus only supplies the place of *i*.

The vowel sounds are *long* or *short*. The short sounds are :—

ă (at), ȧ (ask), a̧ (what); ĕ (end); ĭ (it); ŏ (not), ó (love), o̧ (wolf); ŭ (but), ṳ (pull); and y̆ (hymn).

The pupil can now turn back to Lesson IV., and enunciate the long sounds of each vowel.

The following vowel sounds are compound: namely, that of ī, formed of ä and ï; and that of ū, formed of ĭ and o̱.

Enunciate the two simple sounds together rapidly, and thus produce the compound sound.

The following table shows the long sounds and the corresponding short sounds, with the vowels which represent them:

Long Sounds.			Short Sounds.	
1. ā	ę		ĕ	
2. â	ê		ă	
3. ä			ȧ	
4. a̤	ô		a̤	ŏ
5. ū	ī		ĭ	y̆
6. ē̃	ĩ	ỹ		
7. ō				
8. ǫ	ų		ǫ	ų
9. û			ȯ	ŭ

How many long vowel sounds are there?
By what letters are they represented?
How many short vowel sounds?
By what letters are they represented?
Write a list of words containing each of these sounds.

LESSON VI.

CONSONANT SOUNDS.

The vowels represent *open sounds*.

Open sounds are such as are produced by the organs of speech with a more or less open position of the mouth.

The consonants represent sounds produced by obstructing the vowel sounds, more or less, by means of the lips, teeth, tongue, or palate.

The consonant sounds are sometimes distinguished in pairs, the one kind being called *flats*, and the other *sharps*, as shown in the following table:—

Consonant Sounds.

	Flats.				*Corresponding Sharps.*	
1.	b	as in	bib	p	as in	pip
2.	d	"	did	t	"	toot
3.	ḡ	"	gag	k	"	kin
4.	z	"	zinc	s	"	sun
5.	th	"	the	th	"	thin
6.	v	"	vim	f	"	fin
7.	zh	"	azure	sh	"	ship
8.	l	"	lily			
9.	m	"	mum			
10.	n	"	nun			
11.	r	"	rim			
12.	ng	"	song			
13.	w	"	way			
14.	y	"	yet			
15.	{g / j}	" / "	{gin / jam}	ch	"	church

The consonant *c* represents either the sound of *k*, as in *cat*, or that of *s*, as in *cent*.

The consonant *h* represents merely a breathing, or *aspirate*.

The sound of *g* (soft), or *j*, is not a simple sound, being composed of *d* and *zh*. Its corresponding sharp, *ch* (church), is composed of *t* and *sh*.

There are, therefore, twenty-two simple consonant sounds in English, including the aspirate *h*.

Review.

Of what two kinds are elementary sounds? What is the difference between letters and their powers? Why is a letter made to represent more than one sound? How are vowel sounds represented? How are consonant sounds represented? What are the different sounds of the vowel *a*? What are the sounds of *e*? Of

14 SYLLABLES, DIPHTHONGS, AND TRIPHTHONGS.

i? Of *o?* Of *u?* Of the vowel *y?* Enunciate all the long sounds of each of the vowels. Enunciate all the short sounds. What are diacritical marks? *Ans.* They are marks placed over or under the vowels to distinguish their sound. What vowel sounds are compound? What consonant sounds are compound? What does *h* represent? How are the consonants distinguished? Enunciate the flats. Enunciate the corresponding sharps. How many simple consonant sounds in English?

LESSON VII.

SYLLABLES, DIPHTHONGS, AND TRIPHTHONGS.

When we join letters together, as *p-a, pa; b-o-n, bon,* what do we form?

We form *syllables.*

A **syllable** is one or more letters pronounced in one sound.

When a letter that is not sounded is used in a syllable, it is said to be *mute,* or *silent;* as the letter *e* in *base,* and the letters *u, g,* and *h,* in *though.*

A syllable must have at least one vowel, so as to form a complete sound.

How many vowels are there in *bond?*
How many are there in *bound?*
Do the two vowels in *bound* form one complete sound, or two sounds?

They form only one complete sound, because they are joined together so as to make only one syllable.

There are many other examples of two vowels joined in one sound; as, *oi* in *voice, oa* in *boat, ea* in *beat, ie* in *chief,* etc.

Two vowels joined in one syllable form what is called a **diphthong.**

The syllable *di* (used for *dis*) means *two*, and *phthong* (Greek) means a sound of the voice.

Three vowels are sometimes joined in one syllable; as, *e, a, u*, in *beauty*, and *u, o, y*, in *buoy.*

Three vowels joined in one syllable form what is called a **triphthong.**

From *tri*, three, and *phthong*, a sound of the voice.

In the word *cow* for what vowel is *w* used?

It is used for the vowel *u*.

Other examples are found in *awe, jaw, raw, dew, jew, row, bow, flow, glow,* etc.

What other letter is sometimes a vowel and sometimes a consonant?

When are *w* and *y* consonants?

W and *y* are consonants when they precede a vowel heard in the same syllable; as in *wine, twine, yet, youth.*

LESSON VIII.

DIPHTHONGAL SOUNDS.

Diphthongal Sounds, or sounds of diphthongs, are the following: ōō (long), as in *moon*; ŏŏ (short), as in *book*; *oi* or *oy*, as in *voice* and *boy*; and *ou* or *ow*, as in *loud* and *cow*.

In the diphthong *oa*, as in the word *loaf*, how many of the vowels are sounded?

Only one—the vowel *o*.

In the diphthong *oi* in *voice*, how many of the vowels are sounded?

Both the vowels—ô and ē—which sounded together make the sound *oi*.

A diphthong in which both the vowels are sounded is called a **proper diphthong**.

A diphthong in which only one of the vowels is sounded is called an **improper diphthong**.

Thus *oi* and *oy* are examples of proper diphthongs; and *ea* (in *beat*) and *oa* (in *loaf*) are improper diphthongs.' They have the sounds of single vowels, not *diphthongal sounds*.

A **proper triphthong** is a triphthong in which all the vowels are sounded.

An **improper triphthong** is a triphthong in which only one or two of the vowels are sounded.

Thus *uoy* in *buoy* (pronounced *bwoy*), and *uoi* in *quoit*, are proper triphthongs, and *eau* in *beauty* is an improper triphthong.

Exercises.

1. *Write the following words, one under the other, and at the right of each write the diphthong, or diphthongs, which it contains, with the word* proper *or* improper *after each.*

1. Mean.	7. Builder.	13. Degree.	19. Receive.
2. Chief.	8. Pointed.	14. Coward.	20. Joyous.
3. Goal.	9. Despair.	15. Conscience.	21. Jealous.
4. Reign.	10. Either.	16. Prairie.	22. Nation.
5. Spoon.	11. Ancient.	17. Journey.	23. Tea-spoon.
6. Town.	12. Maintain.	18. Issue.	24. School-boy.

EXAMPLE.—Fountain—*ou* (proper), *ai* (improper).
Fourteen—*ou* (improper), *ee* (improper).

2. *In the same manner, write after each of the following words the triphthong which it contains.*

1. Aweful.	4. Viewless.	7. Anxious.	10. Cautious.
2. Eyelet.	5. Beauteous.	8. Quoiffure.	11. Outrageous.
3. Buoyant.	6. Adieu.	9. Review.	12. Predaceous.

3. *Write a list of five words, each containing one or more proper diphthongs.*

4. *Also five words, each containing one or more improper diphthongs.*

LESSON IX.
SYLLABLES AND WORDS.

How many syllables are there in the word *paper?* In *able?* In *boy?* In *carpenter?* In *clock?* In *egg?*

A **syllable** is either a word or a part of a word.

A **word** is one or more syllables spoken or written as the sign of some idea.

An **idea** is an image or picture in the mind of something previously perceived.

You can think of any object which you have seen—a tree, for example—so as to see it in your mind, like an image or a picture. This mental picture is called an *idea.* The word *tree* enables you to express the idea in speaking or writing. Our thoughts are made up of ideas, and language is the expression of these thoughts.

Words have particular names according to the number of syllables which they contain.

A word of one syllable is called a *monosyllable ;* a word of two syllables, a *dissyllable ;* a word of three syllables, a *trisyllable ;* and a word of four or more syllables, a *polysyllable.*

Mono means one ; *dis,* two ; *tri,* three ; and *poly,* many.

Exercises.

1. *Write a list of ten monosyllables.*
2. *Write a list of ten dissyllables.*
3. *Write a list of five trisyllables.*
4. *Write a list of five polysyllables.*
5. *Write five monosyllables, each containing a diphthong.*
6. *Write five polysyllables, each containing five or more syllables.*

Review.

What is a syllable? What is a diphthong? A triphthong? A proper diphthong? An improper diphthong? A proper triphthong? An improper triphthong? What is a word? An idea? What is a monosyllable? A dissyllable? A trisyllable? A polysyllable?

LESSON X.

DIVISION OF WORDS INTO SYLLABLES.

It is important to know how to divide words into their proper syllables, especially because,

In writing when we come to the end of a line, we may divide a word, but a syllable should never be broken.

The following are examples of words divided into syllables: Harm-less, Con-nect-ed, Con-nec-tion, In-ter-view, Un-doubt-ed-ly, Con-sid-er-a-tion, Im-pos-si-bil-i-ty, Tran-si-to-ri-ness.

The pupil should be required to pronounce these words, enunciating distinctly every syllable.

Of what does each syllable consist?

Each syllable consists of a single vowel, diphthong, or triphthong, and the consonants which belong to it, or modify its sound.

In dividing words into syllables we must be guided chiefly by the ear.

When two vowels come together which do not form a diphthong, they belong to different syllables; as, *a-e-ri-al, co-op-er-ate, zo-ol-o-gy.*

When two vowels come together in this way the fact that they are not a diphthong is indicated by placing two dots (called the *diæresis*) over the second vowel; as, *aërial, coöperate, zoölogy.*

Exercise.

Write the following words, one under the other, and at the right of each write the same word divided into its proper syllables, as in the above examples.

1. Understand.
2. Divisible.
3. Catalogue.
4. Permissible.
5. Aëriform.
6. Degradation.
7. Preparation.
8. Grammarian.
9. Dictionary.
10. Additional.
11. Embarrassment.
12. Monosyllable.
13. Miscellaneous.
14. Orthography.
15. Abecedarian.

LESSON XI.

SIMPLE AND COMPOUND WORDS.

What words are joined together to form the word *watchman?* The words *watch* and *man.*

What words united make *penknife, full-blown, nevertheless?* Words formed in this way from other words are called **compound words.**

Words not composed of other words are called **simple words.**

Thus the words *watch* and *man* are simple words. Compound words are formed by merely placing the simple words together, as in *watchman, nevertheless,* or by joining them with a mark (-) called a hyphen; as in *full-blown, all-wise, schoolboy.*

The hyphen is not used in more common and permanent compounds; as, *moonbeam, horseman, bluebird, penknife, spoonful.*

A **simple word** is one that is not composed of other words.

A **compound word** is one that is composed of two or more simple words.

Exercises.

Write compounds from the following simple words, joining any two that may be properly united, and using the hyphen where required.

Bird, pen, ship, cage, wreck, knife, mouse, moon, beam, trap, shine, sun, day, week, time, mint, pepper, church, box, man, arm, yard, watch, clock, maker, rail, school, road, master.

EXAMPLES.

Bird-cage, penknife, shipwreck, mousetrap.

[In case of doubt as to the use of the hyphen or not, the pupil must be allowed to consult the dictionary.]

LESSON XII.

PRIMITIVE AND DERIVATIVE WORDS.

How is the word *greatly* formed?
By adding the syllable *ly* to the word *great*.

In the same way state how each of the following words is formed:—

1. Connected.
2. Connection.
3. Connective.
4. Connecting.
5. Connector.
6. Disconnect.
7. Connectedly.
8. Unconnected.
9. Connectively.

From what word are all these words formed?
What is a syllable called that is placed after a word, such as *ed, ion, or*, etc.?
It is called a suffix.

What is a syllable called that is placed before a word, such as *dis* and *un?*
It is called a *prefix*.

Which words in the above list have prefixes?
Which have suffixes?
What are words formed in this way called?
They are called **derivative words.**

What are the words called from which they are derived?
They are called **primitive words.**

A **primitive word** is a word not formed from any simpler word.

A **derivative word** is a word derived from some simpler word.

Exercises.

1. *Write five derivative words each containing the suffix* ment.
2. *Write five words each containing one of the following suffixes:* ly, or, ion, less, ard.
3. *Write five words each containing one of the following prefixes:* dis, mis, over, un, under.

4. *Write as many derivative words as you can from each of the following primitive words:* Command, Appear, Construct, Elect, Cover, Press, Inhabit, Destroy.

Write the primitive word in large letters, and underneath, a little to the right, place the derivatives.

EXAMPLE.—**Conceal.**
Concealed.
Concealing.
Concealment.
Unconcealed.

Review.

Into what may words be divided? Of what does each syllable consist? For what is the diæresis used? What is a simple word? What is a compound word? For what is the hyphen used? What is a primitive word? What is a derivative word? What is a prefix? What is a suffix?

LESSON XIII.
SPELLING.

Spelling is the art of expressing words by their proper letters.

This important art is to be acquired by means of the spelling-book or dictionary, by observation in reading, and by the constant use of words in writing. There are, however, a few general rules that are of considerable value, especially in the formation of derivative words.

Primitive words sometimes undergo a slight change when a syllable is added.

Thus when *ing* is added to *please*, the derivative is *pleasing*, the final *e* being dropped. So also when the syllable *ure* is added to *please*, the derivative is *pleasure*. Thus, too, from *force* we have *forced, forcing,* and *forcible ;* and from *love, loving* and *lovable.*

This is expressed in the following—

RULE.—The final *e* of a primitive word should generally be omitted before a suffix beginning with a vowel.

Exception.—When the final e of a primitive word is preceded by c or g, it should be retained before *able* and *ous.*

Because the letters c and g have the hard sounds (as in *cat* and *get*) before a, o, and u, and are soft (as in *cell* and *gem*) before e, i, and y, therefore, to avoid hardening c and g the final e is retained; as, *peaceable, changeable, outrageous,* etc.

Exercise.

Write derivatives from each of the following words, as in the preceding lesson.

1. Lodge.
2. Judge.
3. Cease.
4. Compose.
5. Outrage.
6. Service.
7. Require.
8. Inspire.
9. Courage.
10. Dispose.
11. Agree.
12. Complete.

LESSON XIV.

SPELLING OF DERIVATIVES.

Such monosyllables as *rob, fit, plan, quit,* etc., double the final consonant when the suffix begins with a vowel. Thus:—

Rob—robbing, robbed, robber.
Fit—fitting, fitted, fitter.
Plan—planning, planned, planner.
Quit—quitting, quitted, quittance.

But when the monosyllable has a diphthong, the final consonant is not doubled. Thus:—

Toil—toiling, toiled, toiler.
Heal—healing, healed, healer.

Quit looks like an exception, but it is not, as *u* here performs the office of a consonant, the pronunciation being *kwit*.

When the last syllable of any word contains a single vowel, and the accent falls on that syllable, the final consonant is also doubled. Thus:—

Commit—committing, committed, committee.
Propel—propelling, propelled, propeller.

SPELLING OF DERIVATIVES.

Begin—beginning, beginner.
Acquit—acquitting, acquitted, acquittance.

Accent is the stress placed on a particular syllable in a word, and is sometimes indicated by the mark (′). Thus, permit′, dif′fer.

Hence we have the following—

RULE.—Monosyllables, and words accented on the last syllable, when they end with a single consonant preceded by a single vowel, double the final consonant before a suffix that begins with a vowel.

Exercise.

Write derivatives from the following words, as in the preceding lessons.

1. Dig.	6. Fulfil.	11. Kidnap.	16. Worship.
2. Whip.	7. Peril.	12. Control.	17. Reclaim.
3. Swim.	8. Prefer.	13. Marvel.	18. Annul.
4. Boil.	9. Rebel.	14. Equal.	19. Bedim.
5. Sin.	10. Travel.	15. Occur.	20. Benumb.

LESSON XV.

SPELLING OF DERIVATIVES.—*Continued.*

Primitive words ending in *y* generally change *y* into *i* when a syllable is added. Thus :—

Pity—pitied, pitiless, pitiful.
Merry—merrier, merrily, merriment.

But before *ing*, *y* is retained, to prevent the doubling of *i*. Thus :—

Flying, pitying, decrying, beautifying.

Also, when a vowel precedes the final *y*, it is retained. Thus :—

Gayly, coyness, joyous, enjoyment, moneyed.

Daily, laid, paid, and some others are exceptions.

Words in *ie* drop the *e* by a preceding rule, and change *i* into *y;* as, *die, dying.*

Compound words generally retain the spelling of the simple words that compose them.

But in *permanent compounds* the words *full* and *all* drop one *l;* as, *handful, careful, always, withal.*

Exercises.

1. *Write derivatives from each of the following words, as in the preceding lessons.*

1. Mercy.	5. Deny.	9. Busy.	13. Fancy.
2. Journey.	6. Modify.	10. Plenty.	14. Happy.
3. Beauty.	7. Combat.	11. Defy.	15. Money.
4. Bury.	8. Carry.	12. Annoy.	16. Contrary.

2. *Write the primitive word from which each of the following words is derived, and state what rule is applied in the spelling.*

1. Compelled.	4. Spoonful.	7. Loveliness.
2. Skillful.	5. Preferred.	8. Believing.
3. Happiness.	6. Business.	9. Salable.

That part of grammar which treats of letters, syllables, separate words, and spelling is called **orthography.**

Review.

What is spelling? What is the rule for final *e?* What exception to it? What is the reason for the exception? What is the rule for monosyllables? Exception? What is the rule for doubling the final consonant? What is meant by accent? What is grammar? What is English grammar? What is orthography? *Ans.* Orthography is that part of grammar which treats of letters, syllables, separate words, and spelling.

LESSON XVI.

SYNOPSIS FOR TOPICAL REVIEW.

Orthography.

1. **Language.**
    1. Its purpose.
    2. Different languages.
    3. Ways of using.
    4. Different kinds of.
    5. Simplest elements of.
    6. Grammar.
    7. English grammar.
2. **Letters.**
    1. Forms.
    2. Names, how formed.
    3. Elementary sounds.
    4. Vowels and consonants.
    5. Vowel sounds.
        1. Sounds of *a*.
        2. "   " *e*.
        3. "   " *i*.
        4. "   " *o*.
        5. "   " *u*.
        6. "   " *y*.
        7. Diphthongal sounds.
        8. Sounds of *w*.
        9. Long and short.
        10. How produced.
    6. Consonant sounds.
        1. How produced.
        2. Flats.
        3. Sharps.
        4. Letter *h*.
        5. Number of.
    7. Syllables.
    8. Diphthongs.
        1. Proper.
        2. Improper.
    9. Triphthongs.
        1. Proper.
        2. Improper.
3. **Words.**
    1. Classes.
    2. Monosyllables.
    3. Dissyllables.
    4. Trisyllables.
    5. Polysyllables.
    6. Division into syllables.
    7. Simple.
    8. Compound.
        1. Permanent.
        2. How joined.
    9. Primitive.
    10. Derivative.
        1. Suffix.
        2. Prefix.
    11. Spelling.
        Rules for.

LESSON XVII.

NAMES.

What are such words as *pen, book, pencil, slate?*
They are the *names of things.*

What are *John, William, Eliza, Brown, Smith?*
They are the *names of persons.*

What are *Albany, Buffalo, Philadelphia, New York?*
They are the *names of places.*

Why do we give different names to persons, places, and things?
To distinguish them one from another in speaking and writing.

As we cannot even think clearly of any objects, whether persons, places, or things, and cannot speak or write of them at all, without giving them names, such words are the most important in every language.

Exercises.

Write lists of the following:—

1. Five names of persons.
2. Five names of places.
3. Five names of things.
4. Five names of flowers.
5. Five names of fruits.
6. Five names of animals.
7. Five names of carpenter's tools.
8. Five names of blacksmith's tools.
9. Five names of parts of the body.
10. Five names of parts of a book.
11. Five names of parts of a chair.
12. Five names of things in the school-room.

LESSON XVIII.

SUBJECT AND PREDICATE.

Birds fly. William plays. Trees grow. Horses neigh.

How many statements are here?
Of what does each speak?
What is said of *birds*? Of *William*? Of *trees*? Of *horses*?

Whatever is spoken of is called the **subject**.
What is said of the subject is called the **predicate**.

What are the subjects in the above statements?
Birds, William, trees, and horses.

What are the predicates?
Fly, plays, grow, and neigh.

The subject and predicate joined together make what is called a **sentence**.

In the following sentences, the subject is separated from the predicate. Each may contain one or more words.

Subjects.	*Predicates.*
1. Mary	reads.
2. The sun	shines.
3. The horse	runs swiftly.
4. Bees	make honey.
5. Birds	build nests.
6. The bird	is building a nest.

Exercises.

1. Write predicates for the following subjects:—
Trees ———. Flowers ———. Henry ———. The moon ———.

2. Write subjects for the following predicates:—
——— is writing. ——— sing. ——— bloom. ——— burns. ——— fade. ——— has leaves. ——— is green. ——— shines brightly. ——— falls gently.

LESSON XIX.

THE SENTENCE.

When a subject and a predicate are joined in any way they make **complete sense.**

Any single word serves to express an *idea*, but there must be a subject and a predicate to make the sense complete. Thus each of the following groups of words expresses an idea or a combination of ideas; but, as there is no predicate, the sense is not complete, and none of them is a sentence.

A horse.
A black horse.
A man on horseback.
A horse running away.

In the following, however, there is complete sense:—

The black horse ran away.

What is the subject in this sentence?
What is the predicate?

A **sentence** is an assemblage of words that makes complete sense, and always contains at least one subject and one predicate.

Besides words, there are required in every sentence one or more points, or marks, to express the meaning more clearly.

The following are the principal points, or marks: the Comma [,], the Semicolon [;], the Colon [:], the Period [.], the Dash [—], the Note of Interrogation [?], the Note of Exclamation [!], the Quotation Points [" "], the Marks of Parenthesis—Curves ( ) and Brackets [ ].

The use of these points is called **punctuation.**

Every sentence must end with a period, a note of interrogation, or a note of exclamation.

Exercise.

Copy the sentences given below, separating the subject from the predicate, by a double dotted line, and drawing a straight line under each.

Models.

Birds ======= sing.
The bird ====== sings.
The canary bird ===== sings sweetly.

1. Lions roar.
2. The lion roars.
3. The tawny lion roars terribly.
4. The snow falls slowly.
5. George studies diligently.
6. The diligent pupil improves rapidly.
7. A good servant works faithfully.
8. The winter wind moans dismally.

DIRECTION.—Begin every sentence with a capital letter.

LESSON XX.

THE NOUN AND THE PRONOUN.

The name of any person, place, or thing, when used in a sentence, is called a **noun.**

Point out the nouns in the following sentences:—
The sun shines. The flower blooms. The fire burns.

In the above sentences, is the noun in the subject or in the predicate?

What are the nouns in the following sentences?
Bees make honey. Birds build nests. The sun ripens the fruit. The boy told an untruth.

What nouns are in the subject, and what are in the predicate? John studies. He will improve.

What noun is the subject of the first sentence?
What word is used instead of it in the second?

Alfred has two books. He studies them well.

What nouns in these two sentences?
What words are used for nouns in the second sentence?
For what is *he* used?
For what is *them* used?

A word used instead of a noun is called a **pronoun.**
Pro means *for*, or *instead of*.

Mary gave Mary's book to Mary's brother Charles.

Can you change this sentence by using pronouns so as to avoid repeating the noun Mary?

Mary gave her book to her brother Charles.

Of what use is the pronoun?
It prevents the need of repeating the same noun too often.

Exercise.

Write the following sentences, and fill the blank in each by inserting a pronoun.

1. John lost —— book. 2. Sarah did —— work well. 3. William loves play, and —— will not study —— lessons. 4. The teacher said —— must punish ——. 5. John's mother said to ——, —— must obey ——, or —— shall have to punish ——. 6. The boys said, let —— have some fun. 7. The boy lost —— knife, but —— found —— in —— desk.

LESSON XXI.

THE VERB.

Birds fly. Charles is taught. He is. She sleeps.

Name the predicate in each of these sentences.
What does the predicate *fly* show or express?
It shows what birds *do*, that is, what *action* they perform.

THE VERB.

What does the predicate *is taught* express?
It expresses what is *done to* Charles.
What does the predicate *is* denote?
It denotes *being*, without action of any kind.
What does the predicate *sleeps* denote?
It denotes *being* in a certain *state* or *condition*.

The word in a sentence which shows that the subject is spoken of as *being, acting,* or being *acted upon,* is called a **verb.**

When the name of the person or thing acted upon is in the predicate of the sentence, it is called the **object.**

That is, it is the object upon which the action expressed by the verb is performed; as, "He split the *wood.*" "He felled the *tree.*" "She plucked a *flower.*"

The object answers to the question, what? before the verb. Thus, *He split what? Ans.* The *wood. He felled what? Ans.* The *tree.*

Which is the verb in each of the following sentences, and what does it denote?
In which has the verb an object?
In which is the subject represented as *acting?*
In which as *acted upon?*

1. Cain   slew Abel.
2. Abel   was slain by Cain.
3. The horse.   runs very fast.
4. John   studies his lessons.
5. The boy   was punished.
6. The earth   is a round body.
7. The child   slept soundly.

The **verb** is the principal word in the predicate. The other words in the predicate directly or indirectly depend upon it.

The verb alone may be the predicate. (See *Lesson* XVIII.). Usually other words are required to express fully what we wish to say of the subject. Thus in the sentence *John studies*, we state only how he is employed; but if we wish to say what he studies, we insert the object; and if we desire to state how he studies, we add such a word as *well*, *diligently*, or *carelessly*.

Exercises.

1. *Write three sentences, each containing a verb that denotes* BEING.
2. *Write three sentences, each containing a verb that denotes* ACTION *performed by the subject.*
3. *Write three sentences, in each of which the subject is represented as* ACTED UPON.
4. *Write three sentences, each containing an object.*

Divide each sentence into its subject and predicate, as in *Lesson* XIX.

LESSON XXII.

THE ARTICLE.

The horse ran away. A horse can run.
What do we mean when we say *the* horse?
We mean some particular horse.
What do we mean when we say *a* horse?
We mean *any* horse—no particular horse.

Thus *the* when placed before a noun makes its meaning *definite;* while *a* when placed before a noun shows that it is *indefinite.*

When the noun begins with a vowel *a* must be changed to *an.* Thus we do not say *a apple, a eye,* or *a hour* (*h* being silent), but *an apple, an eye, an hour.* But we say *a union,* not *an union;* because *union* begins with the consonant sound of *y.*

These little words *a, an, the,* are called **articles.**

The is called the **definite article;** and *a* or *an,* the **indefinite article.**

How many articles are there?
What are articles?

Articles are the words *the* and *an* or *a,* which are placed before nouns to limit their signification.

THE ADJECTIVE.

Exercises.

Write three sentences, each containing one or more definite articles.

Write three sentences, each containing one or more indefinite articles.

In each sentence separate the subject from the predicate, as in Lesson XIX.

LESSON XXIII.
THE ADJECTIVE.

A good book instructs. The vicious dog bites.

In each of these sentences, what word is placed before the noun, besides the article?

For what purpose are the words *good* and *vicious* used?

The word *good* expresses the quality of the book; and *vicious*, the quality of the dog.

Words added to nouns to express quality are called adjectives.

How are adjectives like articles?

They are both added to nouns.

How do they differ from articles?

Articles are always placed before nouns; but adjectives are added to nouns, though not always placed before them, and are also added to pronouns. Thus:—

The book is good. *The dog is* vicious. *He is* idle.

Exercise.

Separate the subject from the predicate in the following sentences, as in Lesson XIX.; and draw a line over every article and adjective in each.

1. The old barn was burned.
2. The fierce dog bit the boy.
3. The lightning struck a tall tree.
4. The full moon sheds a pale light.

5. She gave the good scholar a nice new book.
6. The bright sun scorched the green grass.

Review.

What is a sentence? What is the subject of a sentence? What is the predicate? When do words express complete sense? What is a noun? What is a pronoun? Of what use are pronouns? What is the chief word of the predicate? What may the verb express? What is the object? How may it be found? What are articles? How many articles are there? When is *a* used? When is *an* used? How are the two articles named? What words are added to nouns and pronouns? What do they generally express? How do adjectives differ from articles?

LESSON XXIV.
THE ADVERB.

The horse runs swiftly.

What verb is used in the predicate of this sentence?
What word is added to it?
What does the word *swiftly* show?

It shows how, or in what manner, the horse runs.

The horse runs very swiftly.

In this sentence what word is added to *swiftly?*
What does the word *very* show?

It shows how swiftly the horse runs; that is, the *degree* of his swiftness.

I went there yesterday.

What words are added to the verb *went?*
What do they express?

The word *there* expresses place, and *yesterday* expresses time.

Words added to verbs in this way are called **adverbs.**

Adverbs may be added, also, to adjectives or to other adverbs.

Thus, in one of the sentences given above, *very* is added to the adverb *swiftly*. We may say, also, *a very swift horse*, the adverb *very* being added to the adjective *swift*.

Adverbs generally express time, place, degree, or manner.

Exercises.

1. *Copy the following sentences, separating the subject and the predicate in each, as in Lesson XIX., and draw a line over every adverb.*

    1. The sun shines brightly.
    2. The flowers soon fade.
    3. He acted very foolishly.
    4. The old man walks slowly.
    5. Then they went away quickly.
    6. The house is now sold.
    7. I will go there directly.

2. *Write a list of the nouns in these sentences.*
3. *Also of the pronouns, articles, adjectives, and verbs.*

SUGGESTION.—Exercises 2 and 3 may be made oral instead of written exercises at the option of the teacher.

LESSON XXV.
THE CONJUNCTION.

John is a good scholar. William is a good scholar. Charles is a good scholar.

In what respect are these sentences alike?
The predicate is the same in each of them.

Join them together so as to form a single sentence with but one predicate.

John, William, and Charles are good scholars.

What have you joined—subjects or predicates?
What word is used to connect them?
The pupil should observe the use of the comma here.

The pupils read, write, and cipher.

How many verbs are there in the predicate of this sentence? By what word are they connected?

Mary is diligent.   Her sister is idle.

Can you connect these sentences, so as to form only one sentence?

Mary is diligent, but her sister is idle.

What word is used to connect these sentences?

Observe here, also, the use of the comma to separate the connected sentences.

Words used to connect words or sentences are called **conjunctions.**

Exercises.

1. *Write three sentences, each containing a conjunction used in the subject.*

2. *Write three sentences, each containing a conjunction used in the predicate.*

3. *Write three sentences, each composed of two sentences connected by a conjunction, similar to the example given in the lesson.*

4. *Write a list of the conjunctions used in the following sentences, and after each write the words or sentences which they connect.*

   1. Days, months, and years glide away.
   2. Truth endures, but falsehood perishes.
   3. Boys and girls are fond of fun and play.
   4. John failed, because he was careless.
   5. The man was firm, for he was brave.
   6. Samuel and his brothers Henry and James were present.
   7. Scholars should be diligent, earnest, and attentive.

PUNCTUATION.—1. Separate the connected sentences by a comma.   (See 2, 4, 5.)

2. Separate by a comma three or more words of the same kind that form a series.   (See 1 and 7.)

LESSON XXVI.
THE PREPOSITION.

The bird flew over the tree. The boy climbed up the tree. The squirrel ran down the tree.

What verbs are used in these sentences?
To what is the action expressed by each of them related?
It is related to the tree.
Is the relation the same in each?
No; it is *over* the tree in the first, *up* the tree in the second, and *down* the tree in the third.
What words are used to express this relation?
The words *over*, *up*, and *down*.

Words that express relation in this way are called **prepositions.**

A preposition is placed before a noun or a pronoun, and expresses the relation of some other word to it.

Thus, in the above sentences, *over* expresses the relation between *tree* and *flew;* *up*, the relation between *tree* and *climbed;* and *down*, between *tree* and *ran*. This relation is not exactly between the words, but between the *ideas*, expressed by the words.

The noun or pronoun before which the preposition is placed is called its *object*.

The other term of relation is most frequently a verb. Sometimes it is a noun; as, "The *handle* of the knife." Sometimes it is an adjective; as, "*Good* for food."

Exercises.

1. *Write a list of the prepositions in the following sentences, and state the words between which they express the relation.*
   1. The roof of the house leaks.
   2. A pin without a head is useless.
   3. The birds in the tree sing sweetly.
   4. He put the money into the bank.
   5. He gave some money to the beggar.

2. *Write sentences each containing one or more of the following prepositions:* upon, beyond, by, for, of, with, among, under.

LESSON XXVII.
THE INTERJECTION.

My bird is dead. Alas! my bird is dead!

Do both these sentences express the same fact?

How, then, do they differ?

The first merely states the fact, while the other expresses some feeling or emotion with it.

What word is used to denote this feeling?

The word *alas!* which expresses sorrow.

What are words used in this way, to express feeling or emotion, called?

They are called **interjections.**

What interjection is used in each of the following sentences?

1. Oh! how beautiful is the clear sky!
2. Hush! you will disturb her sleep.
3. O, give me back my early days!
4. Pshaw! how ridiculous that is!
5. O! how I long to be free!

Does the interjection form a part of the subject or the predicate of a sentence?

It forms no part of either, but is *independent* of the other words. It is used merely to indicate the emotion caused by the fact or event stated in the sentence.

PUNCTUATION. — Every sentence that expresses emotion should be followed by the exclamation point (!).

The interjection is followed by an exclamation point, except (1) in emotional address, or (2) in expressions which are wholly emotional. As in the following:—

(1) Arise, O Lord! Alas, my noble boy! O ye of little faith!

(2) Ah me! Alas for his family! Oh the grave! the grave!

Exercises.

1. *Write a list of all the interjections which you can think of.*
2. *Write sentences each containing one or more interjections.*

LESSON XXVIII.
THE PARTICIPLE.

Charles flying his kite had a bad fall.
What is the subject of this sentence?
What is added to the noun *Charles?*
The words *flying his kite.*
What does the word *flying* express?
It expresses action, like a verb, and, also, has an object, *kite*, like a verb.
As it is added to the noun *Charles*, what other word does it resemble?
It resembles an adjective.
The word *flying*, therefore, participates in the properties of a verb and an adjective, and is therefore called a **participle.**
Participles sometimes participate in the properties of a verb and a noun.
Thus, in the sentence, "She is fond of reading history," the participle *reading* is the object of the preposition *of*, like a noun, while it expresses action and has an object, like a verb.
How, then, may we define a participle?
A **participle** is a word that participates in the properties of a verb and an adjective, or of a verb and a noun.

The following are examples of the two kinds of participles:—
I. *Verb and adjective.*
   1. The house *taking* fire was destroyed.
   2. My friend *having failed* became poor.
   3. John not *having been promoted* left school.
   4. Arnold, *despised* by all, left the country.
II. *Verb and noun.*
   1. He delighted in *doing* mischief.
   2. He was satisfied with *having done* his duty.
   3. She took pleasure in *being called* amiable.
   4. *Doing* good was her chief occupation.

Participles are derived from verbs. Thus :—

Verbs.	Participles.
Love,	loving, loved.
Walk,	walking, walked.
Kill,	killing, killed.
Go,	going, gone.
Write,	writing, written.

Exercise.

Write a list of the participles in the following sentences, and mention whether they are used as adjectives or nouns.

1. Edgar splitting wood cut his foot.
2. The letter written yesterday was not mailed.
3. Disobeying his parents, John went to the pond.
4. John is very fond of rowing his boat.
5. The men were engaged in mending the road.

LESSON XXIX.

THE PARTS OF SPEECH.

Review.

We have now seen that the words that form a sentence perform different offices. Some are *names;* some express *action* or *being;* some, *quality;* some, *manner* or *time;* some, *connection;* some, *relation*, and others only *emotion*.

The words used in sentences are, therefore, divided into classes called **parts of speech.**

There are ten parts of speech : the Article, the Noun, the Adjective, the Pronoun, the Verb, the Participle, the Adverb, the Conjunction, the Preposition, and the Interjection.

We will here give a simple definition of each.

A **noun** is the name of any person, place, or thing.

An **article** is the word *the, an,* or *a,* which we put before a noun to limit its signification.

REMARK.—There are three words in the English language used as articles, *the, an,* and *a;* but there are, in fact, only two articles, *the* being the definite article, and *an* or *a* the indefinite.

An **adjective** is a word that is added or relates to a noun or a pronoun, and generally expresses quality.

A **pronoun** is a word used instead of a noun.

A **verb** is a word that signifies *to be, to act,* or *to be acted upon.*

An **adverb** is a word added to a verb, an adjective, or another adverb, and generally expresses time, place, degree, or manner.

A **conjunction** is a word used to connect words or sentences.

A **preposition** is a word used to express relation.

An **interjection** is a word that is used merely to indicate some feeling, or emotion.

A **participle** is a word derived from a verb, and participates in the properties of a verb and an adjective, or of a verb and a noun.

That part of grammar which treats of the different parts of speech, and of the classes into which they are divided, is called **etymology.**

What is etymology?

Questions for Review.

What is an adverb? To what may adverbs be added? What is a conjunction? What may conjunctions connect? What is a preposition? What is it placed before? What relation does it express? What is its object? What is an interjection? Is it dependent on any other word? What is a participle? Why so called? Of how many kinds are participles? From what are they derived? What is etymology?

LESSON XXX.

ANALYSIS OF SENTENCES.

A good boy always promptly obeys his parents.

What is the subject of this sentence?
What is the predicate?
What noun forms part of the subject?
What verb forms part of the predicate?
What words are added to the noun *boy?*
What words are added to the verb *obeys?*
What object has the verb?
What pronoun is added to the object *parents?*

The noun *boy*, which is the principal word in the entire subject, is called the **subject noun.**

The subject noun is the subject unmodified by the words added to it.

The verb *obeys*, which is the principal part of the entire predicate, is called the **predicate verb.**

The predicate verb is the predicate unmodified by the words added to it.

The subject noun, or pronoun, and the predicate verb are the principal words of a sentence.

Words added to other words in a sentence are called **adjuncts.**

The word adjunct is derived from the Latin preposition *ad*, meaning *to*, and the Latin participle *junctus*, meaning *joined*.

Thus adjectives and articles are adjuncts of nouns, and adverbs are adjuncts of verbs.

The **analysis of a sentence** is the separation of it into the parts of which it is composed.

This separation is first into its subject and predicate, and then each of these into its principal part and adjuncts.

The following sentence analyzed will afford an example:—
Virtuous youth gradually brings forward accomplished and flourishing manhood.

ANALYSIS.—The subject is *Virtuous youth*, and the predicate the remainder of the sentence. The subject noun is *youth*, and its adjunct is *virtuous*. The predicate verb is *brings*, and its object, *manhood*. The adjuncts of the verb are *gradually* and *forward;* and the adjuncts of the object are *accomplished* and *flourishing*, connected by *and*.

The **use of analysis** is to show how the words in a sentence are related to each other, and what office each of them performs in the sentence.

How may a sentence be built up?

By inserting adjuncts of the subject noun, the predicate verb, and the object of the verb.

EXAMPLE.

Subjects.	Predicates.
The pupil	studies.
The pupil	studies history.
The good pupil	thoroughly studies history.
The industrious pupil	thoroughly studies English history.

What are the adjuncts of the subject noun in the last sentence?
What adjunct has the predicate verb?
What is the adjunct of the object?

Exercise.

Insert adjuncts to the subject noun and predicate verb of the following sentences.

1. The sun shines. 2. The stars twinkle. 3. The wind blows. 4. The lion roars. 5. Horses gallop. 6. The sailor climbs. 7. Snow is falling. 8. The ship sailed. 9. The storm rages. 10. The bird sings. 11. The fox was caught. 12. The ship was wrecked.

LESSON XXXI.

ANALYSIS BY DIAGRAM.

The object of the diagram in the analysis of a sentence is to represent clearly to the eye the structure of the sentence, namely, its entire subject and its entire predicate, and the component parts of each, in their proper relations, as principal parts and adjuncts.

Examples are here given.

DIAGRAM 1.

The | pupil ===== studies ------ history.

What the Diagram Shows.

In this representation, the subject noun and the predicate verb are marked by heavy lines, drawn underneath, separated by a double dotted line, which forms the division between the entire subject and the entire predicate. The object is marked by a light line, and separated from the verb by a single dotted line. The adjunct is written below the word to which it belongs, either at the right or left, according to its proper position, separated from it by a perpendicular line and underscored by a light line. The position of *the* in the above will illustrate this; but it will be more clearly obvious in—

DIAGRAM 2.

The / good | pupil -------- | studies ------ | history.
             thoroughly | English

Exercises.

In the manner shown above, indicate the analysis of the sentences here given.

1. The full moon sheds a soft, pale light.
2. The bright sun scorched the green grass.
3. A diligent pupil always makes rapid improvement.
4. The sharp frost killed the young buds.
5. John carelessly lost his nice new book.
6. The frightened horse ran away swiftly.

LESSON XXXII.

DECLARATIVE AND INTERROGATIVE SENTENCES.

The predicate verb may be a single word or two or more words.

This will be seen in the following sentences: He *went* away. Did he *go* away? He *has gone* away. He *will* not *go* away. Would he *have gone* away?

The words *did, has, will, would, have,* etc., are used to help to express some circumstance connected with the being or action denoted by the verb.

The subject and predicate of a sentence may be combined in several ways: 1. To *declare* some fact; 2. To *ask a question;* 3. To *express an exclamation;* and 4. To *give a command.*

Therefore, sentences are of four kinds: *declarative, interrogative, exclamatory,* and *imperative* sentences.

A **declarative sentence** is one in which the predicate affirms or denies.

An **interrogative sentence** is one in which the predicate asks a question.

Of the above sentences, which are declarative, and which are interrogative?

Sentences are made interrogative by a slight change in the order of the words, or in the form of the predicate verb. Thus:—

Declarative.	*Interrogative.*
1. The moon is rising.	5. Is the moon rising?
2. Henry has gone home.	6. Has Henry gone home?
3. John learns fast.	7. Does John learn fast?
4. William went away.	8. Did William go away?

To analyze an interrogative sentence, first put it in the form of a declarative sentence, but without changing the verb. Thus:—

Did William's brother recite his lessons well to-day?

```
              brother  ........  did recite              lessons.
William's |  ─────── ::::::   ──────────  -------  his  ────────
                                 well                    
                                 to-day
```

Exercise.

Change the following declarative sentences to interrogative sentences, and analyze each by diagram.

1. My father will leave town to-morrow.
2. The European steamer made a short passage.
3. The idle boy did not study his lessons carefully.
4. The diligent pupil will always make great progress.

PUNCTUATION.—Interrogative sentences must always be followed by an interrogation point.

LESSON XXXIII.

IMPERATIVE SENTENCES.

An **imperative sentence** is one that expresses a command or an entreaty.

In imperative sentences the subject is generally omitted. It is understood to be the pronoun *thou* or *you*.

The following are examples of imperative sentences:—

1. Read your book silently.
2. Now go away immediately.
3. Stop that runaway horse.
4. Do not remain away long.
5. John, study your lesson carefully.

The word *John*, in the last of these sentences, simply shows who the subject is. It forms no part of the structure of the sentence, and is, therefore, said to be *independent*.

PUNCTUATION.—The name of a person addressed should be set off by the comma; as, "Tell me, William, if you can."

Exercise.

Write the analysis of the above five imperative sentences in diagram form.

MODEL.

William, perform your task carefully.

```
(You) ------- perform    task.
      carefully    your
[William]
```

The *parenthesis* indicates that the subject is understood; the brackets, that the noun *William* is independent.

LESSON XXXIV.

EXCLAMATORY SENTENCES.

An **exclamatory sentence** is one that expresses some strong emotion, or a mere exclamation.

Exclamatory sentences often contain interjections.
The following are examples of exclamatory sentences:—
1. How fast the horse runs!
2. O! how wrongly you have acted!
3. What a delightful time we had!
4. How wickedly and cruelly some people act!
5. What a bad disposition that boy has!

Very often the words in such sentences need to be *transposed*—that is, placed in the same order as in declarative sentences. Thus, Sentence 4 transposed is, *Some people act how wickedly and cruelly;* and Sentence 5, *That boy has what a bad disposition.*

PUNCTUATION.—Exclamatory sentences should be followed by the note of exclamation. (See *Lesson* XXVII.)

Exercise.

Put in diagram form the above five exclamatory sentences.

MODEL.

"Alas! how shamefully they have treated their friends!"

```
     they  _ _ _ _ _ _ _ _ | have treated    | friends
          how | shamefully |            their |
     [Alas!]
```

Questions for Review.

What is the analysis of a sentence? How is it made? What is the principal part of the subject? Of the predicate? What are adjuncts? How is a sentence built up? How is a sentence analyzed by diagram? In how many ways may the subject and predicate be combined? What is a declarative sentence? An interrogative sentence? An imperative sentence? An exclamatory sentence? What is the punctuation of each? What is the subject of an imperative sentence? What is transposition? When is it needed?

LESSON XXXV.

ORAL ANALYSIS AND PARSING.

After the sentence has been placed in diagram form, the pupil should be required to give an oral analysis of it. The following is an example. (For diagram, see *Lesson* XXXI.)

The good pupil thoroughly studies English history.

Oral Analysis.—This is a declarative sentence. The subject is *the good pupil;* the predicate, *thoroughly studies English history.* The subject noun is *pupil,* and its adjuncts are *the* and *good.* The predicate verb is *studies*, and its adjunct is *thoroughly;* the object is *history*, which has the adjunct *English.*

In a similar manner, give the oral analysis of each of the sentences in the Exercise to Lesson XXXI.

Having discovered by analysis the relations of all the words to each other, and thus the part performed by each in the construction of the sentence, we can easily tell what part of speech each word is, and apply to it the proper rules.

The explaining of each word in a sentence according to the definitions and rules of grammar is called **parsing.**

Analysis applies those principles which belong to every language,—for in all languages there must be subject, predicate, and adjuncts; but parsing recognizes and applies those definitions, rules, and usages that belong to the particular language treated of. Thus below we give the parsing of the above sentence, as far as our progress in the treatment of the subject permits. The parsing will become fuller as we advance; here, of course, it is quite rudimentary.

Parsing.—*The* is an *article*, because it is placed before the noun *pupil* to limit its signification.

Good is an adjective, because it is added to the noun *pupil*, and expresses quality.

Pupil is a noun, because it is the name of a person.

Thoroughly is an adverb, because it is an adjunct of the verb *studies*; it also expresses manner.

Studies is a verb, because it expresses action as performed by the subject *pupil.*

English is an adjective, because it is an adjunct of the noun *history.*

History is a noun, because it is the name of a thing.

Exercise.

Parse in the same manner each word in the sentences given in Lesson XXXI.

[The pupils should be required to give the reason of each statement, as in the above example, so that they may become familiar with the definitions.]

LESSON XXXVI.

THE ATTRIBUTE.

1. *A useful book gives instruction.*
2. *The book is useful.*

Write the analysis of Sentence 1 in diagram.
What adjective is there in the subject.
Why is *useful* an adjective?
Because it is an adjunct of the noun *book*.

What adjective is there in Sentence 2?
Is it in the subject or in the predicate?
It forms a part of the predicate.

Why is *useful* in this sentence an adjective?
Because it relates to the noun book, and expresses quality.

An adjective that relates to the subject, and forms a part of the predicate, is called an **attribute.**

The attribute expresses what is directly affirmed of the subject, or *attributed* to it. Thus, in Sentence 2, the quality of usefulness is attributed to the book spoken of. When we say, *a useful book*, we imply that the book has that quality; but when we say, *The book is useful*, we directly affirm or attribute it. Hence the term *attribute*.

The attribute is not always an adjective, but may be a noun, or a pronoun.

The following sentences afford examples :—

1. Gold is a *metal*.
2. Washington was a true *patriot*.
3. New York is a great *city*.
4. It is *he*.

THE ATTRIBUTE. 51

In Sentence 1, the noun *metal* is an attribute, because it is used as a part of the predicate, and relates to the subject *gold*, since it denotes what gold is; that is, to what class of substances it belongs. The attribute may express class or identity. Thus in 1, 2, and 3, it expresses *class;* in 4, it expresses identity. In the sentence, *She is a queen,* the attribute expresses class; but in, *She is the queen,* it expresses identity.

DIAGRAM OF SENTENCE 3.

New York ----- is | city.
                  a
                  great

The attribute is separated from the verb by a straight line, instead of a dotted line, as in the case of the object. This method of indicating the attribute is followed in all the succeeding diagrams.

Exercise.

Write, in diagram form, the analysis of the following sentences, give the oral analysis of each, and parse each word. State how each noun is used.

1. The sky is blue. 2. The fields are green. 3. My book is old. 4. The spring flowers are very beautiful. 5. Honesty is the best policy. 6. Napoleon was a great general. 7. The tiger is a very ferocious animal. 8. The earth is a spherical body. 9. The boy's industry is quite praiseworthy.

SENTENCE 3—PARSED.

New York is a noun, because it is the name of a place. It is used as the subject noun of the sentence.

Is is a verb, because it signifies being, and is the predicate verb of the sentence.

A is the indefinite article, and relates to the noun *city.*

Great is an adjective, and is added to the noun *city.*

City is a noun, because it is the name of a place. It is used as the attribute in the predicate of the sentence.

LESSON XXXVII.

COMPOUND SUBJECTS AND PREDICATES.

1. *George, William, and Henry took a walk.*
2. *The pupils read, write, and cipher.*

What is the subject of Sentence 1?

It has three subjects, *George, William,* and *Henry,* but they are so connected as to form a single subject.

A subject of this kind is called a *compound subject.*

What is the predicate of Sentence 2?
Is it simple or compound?
What predicate verbs does it contain?

The boys and girls laugh, talk, and play.

What is the subject of this sentence?
What is the predicate?

The diagram here given shows how to represent the analysis of such sentences.

```
                and                         and
       | boys | girls    ------    laugh | talk | play.
  The |
```

This sentence contains in contracted form six sentences: *The boys laugh. The girls laugh. The boys talk. The girls talk. The boys play. The girls play.* The general structure, however, is simple, as the diagram shows.

ORAL ANALYSIS.—This is a declarative sentence, having a compound subject—*The boys and girls*—and a compound predicate—*laugh, talk, and play.* The subject consists of the two nouns *boys* and *girls,* connected by *and, the* being an adjunct of both of them. The predicate consists of the three verbs *laugh, talk,* and *play,* connected by *and.*

Exercise.

In the same manner analyze by diagram and orally each of the following sentences. Also parse the words in each.

1. John and Peter are good scholars.
2. Peaches, pears, and apples are delicious fruit.
3. The animals turned, looked, and ran away.
4. Music cheers, refines, and elevates the mind.
5. Henry, Edward, and Mary attended the same school.
6. John studied well, improved very rapidly, and soon got a good place.

The following diagram of the last sentence will show how the adjuncts are inserted.

```
                        and
  John ...... studied | improved | got ------ place.
               well  | rapidly  |  soon   a
                     | very     |         good
```

PUNCTUATION.—See *Lesson* XXV.

LESSON XXXVIII.

PHRASES.

1. *He did the work* immediately.
2. *He did the work* without any delay.
3. *He did the work* in a short time.

What adverb is added to the verb in 1?
What three words are used for it in 2?
What four words are used for it in 3?

The groups of words, *without any delay* and *in a short time*, perform the same office in 2 and 3 as the word *immediately* does in 1; that is, they are adjuncts of the verb *did*, and express time.

Groups of words of this kind are called **phrases.**

How may we define a phrase?

A **phrase** is a group of words containing neither a subject nor a predicate, and generally performing the office of a single part of speech.

Thus phrases may be used as subjects, objects, attributes, or adjuncts; and, also, as nouns, adjectives, and adverbs. In Sentences 2 and 3, the phrases are, obviously, used as adverbs.

When a phrase begins with a preposition, it is called a **prepositional phrase.**

The object of the preposition is the *principal part* of the phrase.

The principal part of the phrase *without any delay* is *delay;* of the phrase *in a short time* it is *time.* The principal part of a phrase may have a phrase adjunct; as, "In the early part *of the year.*"

Exercises.

Write in diagram form the analysis of the following sentences according to the models given.

MODELS.

1. The kind lady gave some money to that poor man.

```
           | lady ----- gave --------- | money.
    The    |          | to       some |
    kind   |          | man
           |            that
           |            poor
```

2. A pin without a head is wholly useless.

```
        | pin ------ is       | useless.
     A  | | without     wholly|
        | head
      a
```

PHRASES.

The preposition is represented by a perpendicular line joining its object to the word to which the phrase is added, and thus connecting the two terms of relation. Thus *to* expresses the relation between *gave* and *man ;* and *without*, between *pin* and *head.*

ORAL ANALYSIS.—This is a declarative sentence, of which the subject is *a pin without a head ;* and the predicate, *is wholly useless—*
The subject noun is *pin*, and its adjuncts are the article *a* and the prepositional phrase *without a head*, of which *head* is the principal part, having the adjunct *a*.
The predicate verb is *is*, and *useless* is the attribute, having the adjunct *wholly*.

1. The paper lies upon my desk.
2. The cat was sleeping quietly before the fire.
3. A boy without perseverance will always fail.
4. My father will go abroad in the spring of the year.
5. The nimble squirrel swiftly ran up the trunk of the tall tree.

Parse the separate words in each sentence.

go
| in
the ⎰ spring
       ⎱ | of
the | year.

To parse the preposition, mention the words between which it shows or expresses the relation. Thus in the sentence, *A pin without a head is wholly useless*,
Without is a preposition showing the relation between the noun *pin* and the noun *head ;* because the phrase *without a head* is an adjunct of the noun *pin*, being used as an adjective.

Review.

What is parsing?
Ans. Parsing is the resolving or explaining of a sentence according to the definitions and rules of grammar.
How does it differ from analysis? What is an attribute?
Ans. An attribute is an adjective, noun, or pronoun which relates to the subject but forms a part of the predicate.
How is it represented in the diagram? What is a compound subject? A compound predicate? What is a phrase? A prepositional phrase? How is it represented in the diagram? What is the principal part of a prepositional phrase?

LESSON XXXIX.

NOUNS AND THEIR CLASSES.

Thomas, Henry, and George are good boys.

What three nouns form the compound subject of this sentence? How do these nouns differ from the attribute noun *boys*?

The subject nouns are the names of three particular boys, while the attribute noun *boys* denotes the members of a kind or class of persons.

The names of particular individuals are called **proper nouns.**

A proper noun is the name of whatever is particularized, or distinguished as an individual from all others of the same class. Thus the name of a particular people, as the *Romans*, of a particular group of islands, as the *Azores*, or of a range of mountains, as the *Alps*, is a proper noun.

A name that may be applied to any one of a class of beings or things is called a **common noun.**

Common nouns are *general names*, but proper nouns are *particular names*.

Among common nouns are included **collective nouns,** and **participial nouns.**

A **collective noun,** or **noun of multitude,** is the name of many individuals taken together; as, *army, council, meeting, herd, flock*.

A **participial noun** is one formed from a verb, like a participle, but used as a noun; as, "The *triumphing* of the wicked is short."

In the sentence, "The hunting of wild animals is dangerous," *hunting* is a participial noun; but in the sentence, "In hunting wild animals there is danger," *hunting* is a participle.

MODIFICATIONS OF NOUNS.—PERSONS. 57

Exercise.

Analyze by diagram and parse the following sentences. State the class to which each noun belongs.

1. John's brother yesterday went to Philadelphia.
2. A political convention was recently held in Chicago.
3. Columbus sailed from Spain across the ocean.
4. Washington was the first president of the United States.
5. The telling of falsehoods always brings shame.

DIRECTION.—Begin every proper noun with a capital letter.

LESSON XL.

MODIFICATIONS OF NOUNS.—PERSONS.

1. *I, John, wrote the letter.*
2. *William, bring me your slate.*
3. *Samuel has won the prize.*

In what different ways are the nouns *John, William,* and *Samuel* used in these three sentences?

John is used as the name of the person who speaks or writes the sentence; *William,* as the name of the person spoken to; and *Samuel,* as the name of the person spoken of.

The name of the speaker is said to be of the **first person;** that of the person spoken to, of the **second person;** and that of the person spoken of, of the **third person.**

The different ways in which nouns may be used are called **modifications.**

Persons are modifications that distinguish the speaker, the hearer, or person addressed, and the person or thing spoken of.

How many persons are there?
What is the first person? The second person? The third person?

PUNCTUATION.—A noun of the second person should be followed by a comma, and also preceded by it, except when it is the first word in the sentence.

Exercise.

Analyze, classify, and parse all the nouns in the following sentences, stating the class and person of each of the nouns.

1. The book is new. 2. My pen is bad. 3. Charles, come hither. 4. The bird has escaped from its cage. 5. Children, obey your parents. 6. I, Ezra, was there. 7. Samuel, tell the truth. 8. Sarah is a very industrious girl. 9. Mary, study your lessons.

LESSON XLI.
MODIFICATIONS OF NOUNS.—NUMBERS.

The bird sings. The birds sing.
The fox runs. The foxes run.

In these sentences, which nouns signify only one?
Which signify more than one?
How is this indicated?

By adding *s* to *bird*, we form *birds*, which signifies more than one; and by adding *es* to *fox*, we form *foxes*.

Nouns which signify only one are said to be of the **singular number.**

Nouns which signify more than one are said to be of the **plural number.**

Numbers are those modifications which distinguish unity and plurality.

These modifications are marked by a change in the form, or spelling, of the word.

The plural number is generally formed by adding *s* or *es* to the singular.

In most nouns *s* only is added; but when *s* alone will not unite with the singular form, *es* is added; as, *foxes, boxes:* also in some nouns ending in *o;* as, *heroes, mottoes.*

Collective nouns may also be used in the plural; as, *flocks, herds, armies, meetings.*

A change in the spelling of a word to express a modification is called an **inflection.**

A change in the number of the subject noun often requires a change in the form, or spelling, of the verb. (See the sentences at the head of the lesson.)

Exercise.

Write the singular with each of the following plural forms:—

1. Flies.
2. Wives.
3. Knives.
4. Calves.
5. Loaves.
6. Strifes.
7. Feet.
8. Teeth.
9. Chiefs.
10. Geese.
11. Men.
12. Women.
13. Children.
14. Griefs.
15. Pence.
16. Pennies.
17. Axes.
18. Valleys.
19. Sheep.
20. Oxen.
21. Sheaves.
22. Wolves.
23. Duties.
24. Brethren.
25. Mice.
26. Dice.
27. Dies.
28. Handfuls.
29. Mouthfuls.
30. Spoonfuls.
31. Species.
32. Series.

In the word *flies* the *y* of the singular *fly* is changed into *i* according to the rule for such derivatives. (See *Lesson* XV.)

LESSON XLII.

MODIFICATIONS OF NOUNS.—GENDERS.

Father, mother—brother, sister—king, queen—boy, girl— man, woman.

How does each pair of these nouns differ?

One is the name of a male, and the other the name of a female.

MODIFICATION OF NOUNS.—GENDERS.

The modifications of nouns that distinguish the sex which they denote are called **genders**.

The names of males are of the **masculine gender**.

The names of females are of the **feminine gender**.

Which of the above nouns are of the masculine gender? Which are of the feminine gender?

The names of things that are without sex are of the **neuter gender**.

The word *neuter* means *neither*, that is, neither masculine nor feminine.

Of this gender are such nouns as *book, pen, water, truth, knowledge;* that is, the names of *things*, which are neither male nor female.

Names that may be used to denote either males or females are often said to be of the **common gender**.

Of the latter class are such nouns as *parent, child, friend, cousin, person, animal,* etc., which may be applied to a male or a female. They are names that are *common* to both sexes.

How does sex differ from gender?

Sex is the distinction between male and female, but gender is the distinction of nouns in regard to the sex which they denote.

There are four classes of nouns in regard to the sex which they denote: 1, The names of males; 2, The names of females; 3, The names of things without sex; 4, Names that are common to males and females.

The gender of nouns is expressed in three different ways:—

1. By different words; as, *bachelor, maid; boy, girl; buck, doe; bull, cow.*

2. By different inflections, or terminations; as, *abbot, abbess; actor, actress; hero, heroine; janitor, janitrix; executor, executrix.*

3. By compound words; as, *cock-sparrow, hen-sparrow; man-servant, maid-servant; he-goat, she-goat.*

Exercise.

Copy the following list of nouns, and at the right of each write the gender.

1. Soldier.
2. Lawyer.
3. Husband.
4. Vessel.
5. Heroine.
6. Neighbor.
7. Carpenter.
8. Farmer.
9. Parent.
10. Ocean.
11. Bachelor.
12. Building.
13. Servant.
14. Seamstress.
15. Children.
16. Candor.
17. Editor.
18. Cousin.
19. Coachman.
20. Spinster.
21. Captain.
22. Janitrix.
23. Women.
24. Science.

LESSON XLIII.

MODIFICATIONS OF NOUNS.—CASES.

Nouns have another kind of modification, called **cases.**

Cases distinguish the use of the noun as the subject, object, or attribute, or as the name of an owner or possessor.

The subject noun is in the **nominative case.**

The object of a verb, participle, or preposition, is in the **objective case.**

A noun used as the name of an owner or possessor is in the **possessive case.**

Example.—*William gave John's book to Mary.*

In this sentence, *William* is in the nominative case, because it is the subject; *John's* is in the possessive case, because it denotes the possessor, or owner, of the *book;* *book* is in the objective case, because it is the object of the verb *gave;* and *Mary* is also in the objective case, because it is the object of the preposition *to.*

The possessive case does not always imply actual possession or ownership, but sometimes a different though similar relation. It may be represented by various prepositions. Thus: "The man's house," equivalent to, "The house *of* the man."—" Ladies' gloves," or, "Gloves *for* ladies."—"Three years' work," or, "Work *during* three years."—"Homer's poems," or, "Poems *by* Homer."—"Webster's Dictionary," or, "The Dictionary *by* Webster."

The **attribute noun** has the same case as the subject noun.

The case modifications of nouns require no inflections, except that the possessive case is indicated by the addition of *s* with the apostrophe ['] before it.

When the plural form of the noun ends in *s*, the apostrophe only is added.

The following are examples of possessive forms:—

Singular.	*Plural.*	*Singular.*	*Plural.*
1. Friend's,	Friends'.	5. Sheep's,	Sheep's.
2. Man's,	Men's.	6. Prince's,	Princes'.
3. Fox's,	Foxes'.	7. Princess's,	Princesses'.
4. Fly's,	Flies'.	8. James's.	

How many cases are there?
What are they called?
How many and what modifications have nouns?

Exercises.

Show by diagram the analysis of the following sentences, and parse each word, stating the classes and modifications of each of the nouns.

MODEL.

Edgar found in the tree a bird's nest having several pretty eggs in it.

MODIFICATION OF NOUNS.—CASES. 63

PARSING.

Edgar is a proper noun, of the third person, singular number, masculine gender, and the nominative case, because it is the subject of the verb *found*.

Tree is a common noun, of the third person, singular number, neuter gender, and the objective case, because it is the object of the preposition *in*.

Nest is a common noun, of the third person, singular number, neuter gender, and the objective case, because it is the object of the verb *found*.

Bird's is a common noun, of the third person, singular number, common gender, because the name *bird* is common to both sexes, and the possessive case, because it denotes the possession of *nest*.

Eggs is a common noun, of the third person, plural number, neuter gender, and the objective case, because it is the object of the participle *having*.

1. Arnold's treason was fortunately discovered in time.
2. Washington's patriotism preserved the liberty of his country.
3. The teacher told Henry's parents of his misconduct.
4. James's new book was lost somewhere in the street.
5. A true friend will always bear with his friend's infirmities.
6. A faithful servant constantly studies his master's interests.

Review Questions.

Into what two general classes are nouns divided? What is a proper noun? A common noun? What classes are included among common nouns? What is a collective noun? A participial noun? What are modifications? How many modifications have nouns? What are persons? How many persons are there, and what are they called? What is the first person? The second person? The third person? What are numbers? How many are there? What is the singular number? What is the plural number? How is the plural number of nouns formed? What is an inflection? What are genders? What is the masculine gender? The feminine gender? The neuter gender? The common gender? How is the gender of nouns expressed? What is the nominative case? The possessive case? The objective case? In what case is the attribute? How is the possessive case indicated? How may cases be defined?

Ans. Cases are those modifications that distinguish the relations of nouns to other words.

LESSON XLIV.
CONSTRUCTION AND COMPOSITION.

The combination of words into sentences is called **construction.**

Construction is the reverse of analysis. By taking apart properly constructed sentences, we learn how to put them together correctly. Hence the need of practice in both processes.

The combination of sentences to express our thoughts upon any particular subject is called **composition.**

Construct the following:—
1. A sentence containing *a noun, a verb,* and *adjuncts of each.*
2. A sentence containing *a subject noun, a predicate verb,* and *an object* having one or more adjuncts.
3. A sentence with *a subject pronoun,* a *predicate verb,* and an *attribute noun,* with adjuncts.
4. A sentence with an *adjective attribute.*
5. A sentence having one or more *prepositional phrases.*

These sentences which you have constructed do not form a composition, because the thoughts which they express are not related to one another, and do not refer to one particular subject.

The following sentences, all having reference to the same subject, and expressing a connected series of ideas, form a composition upon *Trees.*

TREES.

Trees are beautiful productions of nature. How grand and stately are their forms! How wonderful is their growth! How pleasant is the shade of a thick and wide-spreading oak on a hot summer's day! Have you ever enjoyed this delightful refreshment? The rustling of the leaves in the breeze is sweet music to the ear.

How many sentences are there in this composition?
Of what kind is each?

Write the analysis of each in diagram form.

EXAMPLE.

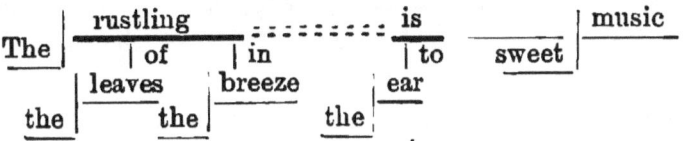

What does the double-dotted line denote? The straight line after the predicate verb? What relation does the preposition *of* express, as shown by the perpendicular line? The preposition *in?* The preposition *to?* How many word adjuncts are there in the sentence? How many phrase adjuncts? What are they?

LESSON XLV.

COMPOSITION.

Write five sentences describing an **elephant.**
Write six sentences about a **lion.**
Write six sentences about a **dog.**
Write several sentences forming a short composition upon **The Cat.**

DIRECTIONS.—1. Do not use the same word too often.

2. Avoid all vulgar, coarse expressions (slang).

3. Mingle long with short sentences, and do not use too many of the latter.

4. Place the adjuncts as near as possible to the words to which they belong.

5. Be careful not to use capitals when they are not required.

6. The letters *I* and *O*, when used as words, should always be capitals.

EXAMPLE OF A FAULTY COMPOSITION.

THE HORSE.

The horse is a large Quadruped he is a useful animal. Some men handle their horses very Fine. Some men are dreadfully cruel to their horses. The Horse can be trained easily and made to work. Most horses are only good to draw big loads. Some horses run awful fast. These are used in Races, & men bet on them. Sometimes they lose a pile of money. Once i rode on a horse and o my, how fast he went. I expect when I grow up i shall get a horse.

FAULTS.—Many words are repeated. There are too many short sentences. Adjectives are used for adverbs, as *fine* and *awful*. There are mistakes in capitals and punctuation; and some of the expressions are coarse and vulgar. The arrangement of ideas may be improved. Compare it carefully with the following.

THE HORSE.

The horse is a large and useful quadruped. He can be easily trained and made to work. Many horses are good only to draw heavy loads, but others are very swift. These are used in the race-course, and men often make large bets upon their speed. Some persons treat their horses with great care and kindness. Others are very harsh and cruel to them. Once I rode upon a horse, and, O, how swiftly I went along! I hope when I have grown up I shall have a horse of my own.

Write similar short compositions on—
The Cow. The Camel. The Whale. The Ship. The Steam-engine. Washington. Columbus. Abraham Lincoln.

The writing of these and similar compositions can be performed while the following lessons are studied, the design being to keep the pupil employed in the actual use of language. The teacher should require the pupils to analyze, as frequently as possible, the sentences of their own compositions.

LESSON XLVI.
CLASSES OF ADJECTIVES.

Some adjectives are used only to describe the quality of persons or things, such as *good, bad, peaceful, warlike;* or their situation, as *eastern, western, outer, inner.*

Such adjectives are called **common adjectives.**

Adjectives formed from proper names are called **proper**

CLASSES OF ADJECTIVES. 67

adjectives; as, *American, English, European, Indian, Washingtonian.*

Adjectives that express a definite, or exact, number are **numeral adjectives;** as, *one, two, three, ten, twenty, twenty-one,* etc.

Numeral adjectives sometimes express numerical order; as, *first, second, third,* etc.

Others express numerical groups; as, *single, double* or *twofold, triple* or *threefold,* etc.

Adjectives sometimes serve only to point out, define, or distinguish, and not to describe, or state the quality of, the person or thing referred to.

Examples of these are *each, both, this,* and *that.*

These adjectives may either be placed before the nouns to which they refer, or may represent them, like pronouns. Thus:—

That (statement) is untrue. *This* (thing) is new. *Both* (persons) are guilty. *Each* (person) confessed.

Adjectives of this kind are called **pronominal adjectives.**

Pronominal means like a *pronoun.*

The following is a list of pronominal adjectives:—

All, any, both, each, either, every, few, former, first, latter, last, many, neither, none, one, other, same, some, such, this, that, which, and *what.*

What is a pronominal adjective?

A **pronominal adjective** is a definitive word which may either accompany its noun or represent it understood.

Definitive words are words that serve to define, limit, or distinguish; such as articles and the adjectives called *pronominal.*

Adjectives that have the form of participles are called **participial adjectives.**

Participial adjectives differ from participles in not at all partaking in the nature of the verb. They merely describe, or express quality; as, "A *trying* position."—"A *waxed* thread."—"The *rising* sun."—"A *frozen* river."

In the sentence, *A running horse will sometimes stumble*, the word *running* is an adjective; but in the sentence, *A horse running rapidly stumbled*, the word *running* is a participle.

Adjectives that consist of two or more words joined by a hyphen are called **compound adjectives**; as *four-footed, fresh-looking, dark-eyed.*

How many kinds of adjectives are there?
What are they called?

Exercises.

1. *Classify the adjectives in the following expressions.*

Write the adjective, and after it the name of the class to which it belongs.

1. Good children.
2. Pleasant weather.
3. Interesting books.
4. Roman soldiers.
5. Triple time.
6. Charming music.
7. Barking dogs.
8. The French language.
9. A single person.
10. The seventh king.
11. The same person.
12. Such is the fact.
13. All are responsible.
14. This is true.
15. The Austrian government.
16. Shakspearean style.
17. The nineteenth century.
18. Those poor persons.
19. Old-fashioned dresses.
20. Both are bad boys.
21. The last Roman king.

2. *Write sentences each containing an example of one or more classes of adjectives.*

DIRECTION.—Proper adjectives, like proper nouns, should begin with a capital letter.

LESSON XLVII.

COMPARISON OF ADJECTIVES.

Adjectives are varied in form in order to express the different degrees of quality in objects compared with one another.

Thus we may say: "Iron is *heavy*, lead is *heavier*, but gold is the *heaviest* of these three metals; while platinum is the *heaviest* of all metals."

The variation of the form of the adjective to express quality in different degrees is called **comparison**.

There are three degrees of comparison; the **positive,** the **comparative,** and the **superlative.**

The **positive degree** is expressed by the adjective in its simple form.

Thus *heavy*, in the above sentence, is of the positive degree. The quality of *heaviness* as existing in iron is taken as a standard of comparison with the other metals referred to.

The **comparative degree** is that which exceeds the positive.

Thus we say, "Lead is *heavier* than iron; gold is *heavier* than lead; but platinum is *heavier* than gold." The comparative degree can be used only when *two objects* are compared.

The **superlative degree** is that which is not exceeded.

The superlative degree implies the comparison of *three or more objects*, and expresses a superiority to all others compared.

Thus gold is the *heaviest* of the three metals, iron, lead, and gold, but platinum is the *heaviest* of all metals.

The **regular form of comparison** is by adding to the positive *er* to form the comparative, and *est* to form the superlative. Thus:—

Positive.	Comparative.	Superlative.
hard	harder	hardest
wide	wider	widest
hot	hotter	hottest
simple	simpler	simplest

As will be seen, when the positive ends in *e*, *r* only is added.

There are several irregular modes of comparison; as, *good, better, best; bad* or *ill, worse, worst; little, less, least; much* or *many, more, most; far, farther, farthest; late, later* or *latter, latest* or *last.*

Only monosyllables and dissyllables which end in *y* or mute *e* can, with few exceptions, be regularly compared.

Other adjectives are compared by using the adverbs *more* and *most;* as, *virtuous, more virtuous, most virtuous.* This is, of course, not a variation of the adjective.

Diminution of quality is expressed by the adverbs *less* and *least.* Thus: *diligent, less diligent, least diligent.*

Adjectives that do not express quality cannot be compared, nor any adjective whose signification does not admit of degrees; as, *central, equal, total, perfect, infinite, eternal.*

The termination *ish* is sometimes used to imply a quality inferior to the positive; as, *reddish,* meaning *somewhat red.*

The adjectives *this* and *that* change their form to express the plural number. Thus, *this man, these men; that book, these books.*

Exercise.

Write the comparison of the following adjectives, regularly, irregularly, or by means of adverbs, as each may require.

1. Short.
2. Soft.
3. Small.
4. Late.
5. Few.
6. Happy.
7. Many.
8. Noble.
9. Gentle.
10. Famous.
11. Early.
12. Little.
13. Narrow.
14. Useful.
15. Unkind.
16. Wicked.
17. Pleasant.
18. Idle.
19. Ill.
20. Severe.
21. Amiable.
22. Amusing.
23. Agreeable.
24. Elegant.

LESSON XLVIII.

SIMPLE AND COMPOUND SENTENCES.

Any combination of the subject and predicate forms what is called a **proposition.**

A **simple sentence** is one that contains only a single proposition.

EXAMPLES.—Riches have wings.—I laugh and weep.—The sun and moon give us light.

In each of these sentences there is but one *proposition* or combination of subject and predicate, though in some there may be more than one subject noun or predicate verb, since the subject or predicate of a proposition may be simple or compound. (See *Lesson* XXXVII.)

A **compound sentence** is one that is composed of two or more simple sentences, connected by a conjunction.

EXAMPLES.

1. Art is long, and time is fleeting.
2. Home is home, though it be ever so homely.
3. Life is short, but it is followed by eternity.
4. Virtue is its own reward, and vice brings its own punishment.
5. Hatred stirreth up strifes, but love covereth all sins.
6. The tulip is a gorgeous flower, the lily is a beautiful one, but the rose is the fairest of all.

A sentence that forms a part of a sentence is called a **clause.**

How many clauses are there in each of the above sentences?

Exercise.

Write in diagram form the analysis of each of the above sentences; analyze them orally, and parse the words in each. (See example of written exercise below.)

SIMPLE AND COMPOUND SENTENCES.

EXAMPLE ANALYZED.

"Avoid not the struggle for truth, though it be ever so formidable."

```
(Thou or you) ---- avoid  |                  | struggle
                          | not       the|   | for      though
                  it ---- be            formidable.     truth
                              |  so
                              ever
```

The pupil will observe how the secondary adjunct *ever* (adjunct of an adjunct) is represented.

ORAL ANALYSIS.—This is a compound imperative sentence, consisting of the clauses, *Avoid not the struggle for truth*, and *be it ever so formidable*, connected by the conjunction *though*. The separate clauses are to be analyzed as in preceding examples.

WRITTEN EXERCISES IN PARSING.

The following affords a model for these exercises.

Word.	Part of Speech.	Class.	Modifications.	Relation.
Avoid	Verb.			Predicate.
Not	Adverb.			Adj't of *avoid*.
The	Article.	Def.		Adj't of *truth*.
Struggle	Noun.	Com.	3d, Sing., N., Obj.	Obj. of *avoid*.
For	Preposition.			*Struggle* and *truth*.
Truth	Noun.	Com.	3d, Sing., N., Obj.	Obj. of *for*.
Though	Conjunction.			Cong. clauses.
It	Pronoun.			Sub. of *be*.
Be	Verb.			Pred. of 2d clause.
Ever	Adverb.			Adj't of *so*.
So	Adverb.			Adj't of *formidable*.
Formidable	Adjective.			Att. after *be*.

Questions for Review.

What is construction? What is composition? How many classes of adjectives? What are they? What is a common adjective? *Ans.* A common adjective is one that simply denotes quality or situation. What is a proper adjective? A numeral adjective? A pronominal adjective? A participial adjective? A compound adjective? What is comparison? How many degrees of comparison? Positive degree? Comparative degree? Superlative degree? What is the regular form of comparison? What adjectives can be regularly compared? What adjectives vary their form to express the plural? What is a proposition? A simple sentence? A compound sentence? A clause?

LESSON XLIX.

CLASSES OF PRONOUNS.

Pronouns have the same modifications as nouns; namely, **persons, numbers, genders,** and **cases.**

Some pronouns show by their form that they are of the first, second, or third person.

Thus the pronoun *I* always stands for the speaker; *thou*, for the person spoken to; and *he, she,* or *it,* for the person or thing spoken of.

A pronoun that shows by its form of what person it is, is called a **personal pronoun.**

The personal pronouns are **I, thou, he, she,** and **it,** with their variations.

When a pronoun is used in one clause of a sentence to represent a noun or pronoun in a preceding clause, and thus connects the clauses, it is called a **relative pronoun.**

The word which the relative pronoun represents, or to which it relates, is called its **antecedent.**

Thus in the sentence, *The flowers which bloom in the spring are beautiful,* there are two clauses: *The flowers are beautiful,* and *which bloom in the spring.* The word *which,* representing the antecedent word *flowers,* is the subject of the second clause; and in this way it serves to connect the two clauses. Hence we may give the following definition of a relative pronoun :—

A **relative pronoun** is a pronoun that represents an antecedent word, and connects different clauses of a sentence.

The person, number, and gender of a relative pronoun are the same as those of the antecedent word which it represents.

The simple relative pronouns are, *who, which, what*, and *that.*

The words *who, which,* and *what* are also used in asking questions, and are then called **interrogative pronouns;** as, " *Who* is there?"—" *What* did you say?"—" *Which* will you have?"

There are, therefore, three classes of pronouns; namely, **personal, relative,** and **interrogative.**

Who is usually applied to persons only; **which,** though formerly applied to persons, is now confined to brute animals and inanimate things; **what,** as a mere pronoun, is applied to things only; **that** is applied indifferently to persons, animals, and things.

Exercise.

Write in diagram form the analysis of the sentences given below; and write in the form prescribed in the preceding lesson the parsing of each word, classifying the pronouns.

Model.

Napoleon, who made so many conquests, was during six years a captive in St. Helena.

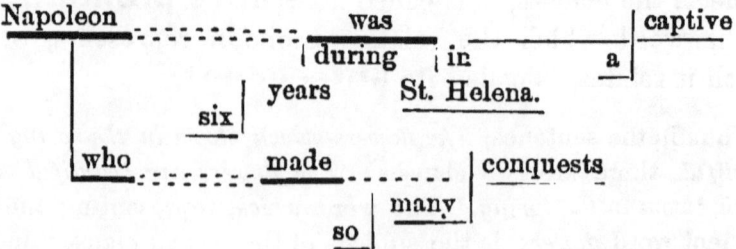

DIFFERENT FORMS OF PRONOUNS. 75

ORAL PARSING.— *Who* is a relative pronoun, the antecedent of which is *Napoleon*, and is, therefore, of the third person, singular number, and masculine gender; and it is in the nominative case, because it is the subject of the verb *made*.

1. Washington, who was a true patriot, is admired by all.
2. Arnold, who betrayed his country, is universally despised.
3. James's book, which was given to him by his father, was lost.
4. I, who saw the whole affair, will explain it fully.
5. Jupiter, which is the largest of the planets, has four satellites.
6. Rome, which was once the mistress of the world, was pillaged by the barbarous Vandals.

LESSON L.

DIFFERENT FORMS OF PRONOUNS.

The modifications of personal pronouns are expressed by variations of form, or by different words.

Thus the pronoun of the first person, singular number, is *I* in the nominative case, and *me* in the objective case; but in the plural number it is *we* in the nominative case, and *us* in the objective case.

A regular arrangement of these forms, according to number and case, is called **declension**.

Declension of the Personal Pronouns.

I, of the *first person.*

Sing. *Nom.* I.
    Poss. my, *or* mine,
    Obj. me;

Plur. *Nom.* we,
    Poss. our, *or* ours,
    Obj. us.

Thou, of the *second person.*

Sing. *Nom.* thou,
    Poss. thy, *or* thine,
    Obj. thee;

Plur. *Nom.* ye, *or* you,
    Poss. your, *or* yours,
    Obj. you.

He, of the *third person.*

Sing. *Nom.* he,
Poss. his,
Obj. him;

Plur. *Nom.* they,
Poss. their, *or* theirs,
Obj. them.

She, of the *third person.*

Sing. *Nom.* she,
Poss. her, *or* hers,
Obj. her;

Plur. *Nom.* they,
Poss. their, *or* theirs,
Obj. them.

It, of the *third person.*

Sing. *Nom.* it,
Poss. its,
Obj. it;

Plur. *Nom.* they,
Poss. their, *or* theirs,
Obj. them.

The pupil should observe that the plural forms of *he, she,* and *it* are the same.

The *gender* is distinguished by the form only in the third person singular. All the other forms are common; that is, the forms *they, their* or *theirs,* and *them* are used to represent nouns whether masculine, feminine, or neuter.

Of the relative and interrogative pronouns, *who* is the only one that changes its form, becoming *whose* in the possessive case, and *whom* in the objective. These forms are both singular and plural.

That, which, and *what* cannot be used in the possessive case. The phrase *of which* is used instead of the possessive; as, "He found a watch the owner *of which* was not known."

Exercises.

1. *Write the nominative plural of* I, thou, he, she, it.
2. *Write the objective singular of the same.*
3. *Write the possessive singular and plural of each.*
4. *Write five simple sentences, each containing one of the objective plural forms of the simple personal pronouns.*
5. *Write sentences each containing* mine, thine, ours, yours, *or* theirs.
6. *Write three sentences, each containing the pronoun* whose.

LESSON LI.

COMPOUND PERSONAL PRONOUNS.

The **compound personal pronouns** are *myself, thyself, himself, herself,* and *itself.*

These pronouns are not used at all in the possessive case, and in the nominative and objective have the same form. They differ only in the singular and plural. Thus:—

Sing. myself, thyself,   himself, herself, itself.

Plur. ourselves, yourselves,   themselves.

As *you* generally takes the place of *thou, yourself* is used in the singular number for *thyself;* as, "You (sing.) have condemned *yourself.*"—"You (plural) must respect *yourselves.*"

The compound personal pronouns are used when the object or attribute refers to the same person or thing; as, "I defended *myself.*"— "He injured *himself.*"—"The man was not *himself* at the time."

A preposition sometimes intervenes; as, "He spoke for *himself.*"—"She took it upon *herself.*"

Sometimes they are used only for emphasis; as, "He *himself* is to blame."—"We *ourselves* are guilty."

Exercises.

1. *Write three simple sentences, each containing one of the compound personal pronouns of the singular number.*

2. *Write three simple sentences, each containing a compound personal pronoun of the plural number.*

3. *Analyze by diagram the following sentences, and write the parsing.*

1. He gave himself up to vicious indulgences.

2. Good persons will often sacrifice themselves for the benefit of others.

3. The unhappy mother greatly censured herself for her carelessness.

4. We should keep a constant watch upon ourselves, if we would avoid errors of conduct.

5. They rashly and weakly surrendered themselves to the enemy upon the first attack.

6. Remorse for evil conduct resembles the fabled scorpion, for it stings itself to death.

Questions for Review.

What modifications have pronouns? How many classes of pronouns are there? What is a personal pronoun? A relative pronoun? An interrogative pronoun? What are the simple personal pronouns? The compound personal pronouns? The simple relative pronouns? The interrogative pronouns? How are the relative pronouns applied? What is declension? Decline each of the simple personal pronouns. Which of the relative pronouns changes its form? What variations have the compound personal pronouns? How are they used?

LESSON LII.

DIFFERENT KINDS OF ADJUNCTS.

Adjuncts may be words, phrases, or clauses. Thus:—
1. A *truthful* boy is believed.
2. A boy *of truth* is believed.
3. A boy *who tells the truth* is believed.

In Sentence 1, the subject noun, *boy*, has a word adjunct, *truthful;* in 2, it has a phrase adjunct, *of truth;* and in 3, it has a clause adjunct, *who tells the truth.* Each of these is an *adjective adjunct*, having the same meaning.

Adjuncts modify, describe, or explain, and are, accordingly,

DIFFERENT KINDS OF ADJUNCTS.

called **modifying adjuncts, descriptive adjuncts,** or **explanatory adjuncts.**

The following are examples:—

Modifying Adjuncts.	Descriptive Adjuncts.
1. An *honest* man.	5. The *sagacious* elephant.
2. The *brave* soldier.	6. The *busy* bee.
3. A man *of integrity.*	7. The owl, *fond of darkness.*
4. A boy *who is studious.*	8. John, *who is studious.*

A **modifying adjunct** is one used to distinguish the person or thing named from others of the same class or kind.

A **descriptive adjunct** is one that describes an individual, or expresses a quality that belongs to all of the same class or kind.

In the above examples, the adjuncts *honest* and *brave* express qualities that do not belong to all men or all soldiers; but *sagacious* and *busy* are common to the whole class, for all elephants are *sagacious,* and all bees are *busy;* as all owls are *fond of darkness.* The clause *who is studious* modifies *boy,* because it serves to distinguish him from other boys; but when it is applied to the proper noun *John,* it merely describes him as an individual.

An **explanatory adjunct** is a noun, pronoun, phrase, or clause used to explain a preceding noun or pronoun.

The following sentences contain examples:—

1. Is your sister *Mary* present?
2. Nero, *the Roman emperor,* was very cruel.
3. How can I, *your brother,* help you?
4. It is very useful *to study grammar.*
5. It is not proper *that you should go.*

In Sentence 1, the noun *Mary* is an explanatory adjunct of *sister;* in 2, the phrase *the Roman emperor* is an explanatory adjunct of Nero; in 3, *your brother* is an explanatory adjunct of *I;* in 4, the phrase *to study grammar* is an explanatory adjunct of the pronoun *it;* and in 5, the clause *that you should go* is explanatory of *it.*

Explanatory adjuncts are said to be in **apposition** with the noun or pronoun which they explain.

PUNCTUATION.—1. Descriptive phrase or clause adjuncts should be separated by the comma.

2. Explanatory adjuncts should be separated by the comma (see Sentences 2 and 3); but not when the word and its adjunct (as in Sentence 1) form a single name or phrase, or in such phrase or clause adjuncts as those in 4 or 5.

Exercises.

1. *Classify the adjuncts in the following phrases, and write a list of each.*

1. An obedient child. 2. The fierce tiger. 3. An industrious man. 4. The sly cat. 5. Mortal men. 6. A man of energy. 7. William, my brother. 8. My brother Charles. 9. Man, who is mortal. 10. Sinful men. 11. Hope, that never leaves us. 12. Cowper, the poet. 13. We, who are innocent. 14. A boy who loves to study. 15. Life, that is so short. 16. Fleeting time.

2. *Write sentences containing one or more of these phrases, and punctuate as directed.*

3. *Analyze by diagram each of the phrases.*

MODELS.

Man, who is mortal.   William, my brother.

The double straight perpendicular line always indicates an explanatory adjunct, or the relation called apposition.

LESSON LIII.

ADVERBIAL ADJUNCTS.

An **adverbial adjunct** may be a word, a phrase, or a clause. Thus :—

1. The work was done *promptly*.
2. The work was done *in a short time*.
3. The work will be done *when I have the time*.

What is the adverbial adjunct in Sentence 1?
What phrase is used as an adjunct in 2?
What clause is used as an adjunct in 3?

A clause used as an adjunct is called a **dependent clause.**

A dependent clause may also be used as the subject, object, or attribute of a sentence.

EXAMPLES.

1. (Subject).—That *the earth is round* is well known.
2. (Object).—Columbus believed that *the earth is round*.
3. (Attribute).—His belief was that *the earth is round*.
5. (Adjunct).—He believed it more strongly when *he landed on St. Salvador*.

The clause upon which another clause depends is called the **principal clause.**

The clauses of a sentence that are connected merely by conjunctions without dependence are called **independent clauses.** (See Examples in *Lesson* XLVIII.)

In Sentence 3, *The work will be done* is the principal clause, and *when I have the time* is the dependent clause, this clause being used as an adjunct of the predicate verb *will be done*. The adverb *when* is an adjunct of *have*, and serves to connect the two clauses. This is illustrated in the following diagram.

COMPLEX SENTENCES.

[Diagram: The *work* = will be done / when I = have — time. / the]

Adverbs that connect the clauses of a sentence are called **conjunctive adverbs.**

There are several words used as conjunctive adverbs: as, *when, where, after, before, since,* etc.

Exercise.

Put in diagram form the following sentences :—

1. Where is your book? (Transpose first into, Your book is where?)
2. At what place did you leave it?
3. When did you use it last?
4. Seek for it where you left it.
5. Can you not find it in your desk?
6. It was taken away after I left it there.
7. I will find it before I come back.
8. I hope that I shall not be disappointed.

LESSON LIV.

COMPLEX SENTENCES.

A sentence that is composed of a principal clause, and one or more dependent clauses, is called a **complex sentence.**

Compound sentences are composed of independent clauses. (See *Lesson* XLVIII.)

A clause introduced by a relative pronoun is called a *relative clause.* Relative clauses are always adjective adjuncts.

The examples given in *Lesson* XLIX. are all descriptive clauses;

COMPLEX SENTENCES. 83

the sentences given below contain examples of both modifying and descriptive adjuncts.

PUNCTUATION.—Relative clauses when modifiers should not be preceded by the comma. (See *Lesson* XLIX.)

EXAMPLES OF COMPLEX SENTENCES.

1. Children who disobey their parents deserve punishment.
2. He that walketh uprightly walketh surely.
3. Cæsar, who won so many victories, was assassinated.
4. Reverence your parents, from whom you have received so many benefits.
5. The event which was predicted long before has occurred in a surprising manner.
6. Can a boy that habitually tells falsehoods be trusted by any one?
7. How beautiful was the prospect upon which we then gazed!

EXAMPLE 7, ANALYZED.

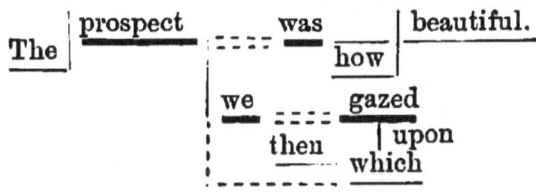

This diagram is designed to represent that the clause, *upon which we then gazed*, is used as an adjunct of the noun *prospect*, while the phrase *upon which* is an adjunct of the verb *gazed*. The dotted line in continuation of the adjunct line shows the connective and relative character of the pronoun.

ORAL ANALYSIS.—This is a complex exclamatory sentence, of which *How beautiful was the prospect* is the principal clause, and *upon which we then gazed* is the dependent clause, being used as an adjunct of the noun *prospect*. [Each clause to be analyzed as in the preceding examples.]

Exercises.

1. *In a similar manner analyze, by diagram and orally, each of the above sentences.*

2. *Prepare a written parsing exercise of Sentences* 1 *and* 2. (See *Lesson* XLVIII.)

LESSON LV.

CONSTRUCTION.—REVIEW.

1. *Write three compound sentences, each consisting of two simple clauses connected by* and *or* but.

EXAMPLE.—John is diligent, but his brother is idle.

2. *Write three complex sentences, each containing a relative clause.*

For examples see *Lessons* XLIX. and LIV.

PUNCTUATION.—1. The simple clauses composing a compound sentence should be separated by a comma.

2. The relative clause should be preceded and followed by a comma, except when it is a modifying clause.

3. *Write complex sentences, each containing one of the following used as an adjunct clause.*

1. When summer comes. 2. While I was away. 3. Which his mother gave him. 4. That I ever saw. 5. Before he came here. 6. Until his father returned.

4. *Insert a relative clause to fill the blank in each of the following sentences.*

1. The book —— was lost. 2. He would not learn the lesson ——. 3. The horse —— was caught by a policeman. 4. Time —— can never be regained. 5. He —— is guilty of great wrong. 6. The bee —— stung his hand. 7. Charles caught the bird ——.

Questions for Review.

What may be used as adjuncts? Of how many kinds are adjuncts? What is a modifying adjunct? What is a descriptive adjunct? An explanatory adjunct? An adverbial adjunct? What is a dependent clause? What is the principal clause? What are independent clauses? What are conjunctive adverbs? What is a complex sentence? What is a relative clause? When does a relative clause require the comma?

LESSON LVI.

CONSTRUCTION.—*Continued.*

When a relative clause is a modifying adjunct it can usually be changed to an adjective or participle, thus changing the complex sentence into one that is simple.

Thus we may change the complex sentence, *A pupil who is diligent will excel,* into the simple sentence, *A diligent pupil will excel.*

Sometimes a phrase consisting of a noun and an adjective may be used instead of a relative clause and the antecedent.

Thus, *He who labors faithfully will succeed,* may be changed to, *A faithful laborer will succeed.*

Change the following complex into simple sentences, by either of the above methods.

1. A man who acts honorably will be respected.
2. Children who are stubborn are controlled with difficulty.
3. A figure that has three sides is called a triangle.
4. He who studies faithfully will gain knowledge.
5. They who do wrong repent of it, sooner or later.

When the relative clause is not a modifying adjunct, the complex sentence may be made compound, by using a personal pronoun and an adjective for the relative.

Thus, *John, who won the prize, worked very hard,* may be changed to, *John worked very hard, and he won the prize.* Or, we might say, *John won the prize, but he worked very hard for it.*

Change in this manner the following complex to compound sentences, using the conjunction indicated for each case.

1. Mr. Smith, who was ill, has recovered. [*But.*]
2. Washington, who was a true patriot, saved his country. [*And.*]
3. William, who has told so many falsehoods, cannot now be believed. [*Because.*]
4. I, who was wholly innocent, was condemned. [*Though.*]
5. You, who know nothing of it, are suspected. [*And yet.*]

LESSON LVII.

COMPOUND RELATIVE PRONOUNS.

1. *He who does wrong will suffer.*
2. *Any one who does wrong will suffer.*
3. *Whoever does wrong will suffer.*

In the Sentences 1 and 2, which is the principal and which the dependent clause?

How many clauses are there in Sentence 3?

There are two clauses, the word *whoever* being equivalent to *he who* or to *any one who;* that is, to both the antecedent and the relative.

The following sentences contain words used in the same way:—

1. *Whoever,* or *whosoever,* does wrong will surely repent of it.
2. *Whomever,* or *whomsoever,* he found trespassing he punished.
3. *Whichever,* or *whichsoever,* you desire I will give you.
4. *Whatever,* or *whatsoever,* you request you will obtain.
5. His father will cheerfully give him *what* he needs.

EXPLANATION.—In Sentence 1, *whoever* or *whosoever* is equivalent to *he who.* It is both the antecedent and the relative. In 2, *whomever* or *whomsoever* is the same in meaning as *him whom.* (*He punished whomsoever he found.*) In 3, *whichever* or *whichsoever* is the same as *that which* or *anything which.* In 4, *whatever* or *whatsoever* has the same meaning.

The words *whoever* or *whosoever, whichever* or *whichsoever,* and *whatever* or *whatsoever* are called **compound relative pronouns.**

The relative pronoun *what,* though simple in form, is compound in office. (See Sentence 5.)

COMPOUND RELATIVE PRONOUNS.

Compound relative pronouns are such as have a twofold relation, or office, serving for the antecedent in one clause of a sentence and for the relative pronoun in the other.

Exercise.

Analyze in diagram form the five sentences given above. Parse the separate words, orally or by written exercise.

MODEL.

Always do whatever your parents command.

(You) ---- | do --- whatever --- parents ==== command.
always | your

The double line underneath *whatever* indicates its twofold relation to the clauses. The dotted line before *whatever* denotes that the clause is the object of the verb *do;* and that following it denotes that it is the object in its own clause.

ORAL ANALYSIS.—A complex imperative sentence, consisting of two clauses, of which *Always do* is the principal clause, and *whatever your parents command* is the dependent clause, being the object of the verb *do.*

ORAL PARSING.—*Whatever* is a double relative pronoun, of the third person, singular number, neuter gender, and the objective case, being the object of the verb *command*, in the object clause. (It may be also considered as the object of both the verbs *do* and *command;* or may be analyzed into the antecedent *that* and the relative *whichever*, the former being the object of *do*, and the latter of *command.*)

WRITTEN PARSING.

Word.	Part of Speech.	Class.	Modification.	Relation.
Always	Adverb.	Of time.		Adj't of *do.*
Do	Verb.			Pred. Verb.
Whatever	Pronoun.	Comp. Rel.	3d, Sing., Neut., Obj.	Obj. of *command.*
Your	Pronoun.	Personal.	2d, Pl., Com., Poss.	Adj't of *parents.*
Parents	Noun.	Common.	3d, Pl., Com., Nom.	Sub. of *command.*
Command	Verb.			Pred. Verb.

LESSON LVIII.

DIFFERENT KINDS OF VERBS.

A verb represents its subject as *being, acting,* or *being acted upon.*

A verb that represents its subject as *being* is called a **neuter verb;** as, I *am.*—He *sleeps.*

A verb that represents its subject as *acting* is called an **active verb;** as, I *write.*—He *walks.*

A verb that represents its subject as *being acted upon* is called a **passive verb;** as, I *am compelled.*

The word *passive* means *suffering* or *enduring.* As applied to a verb, it is the opposite of *active;* that is, *inactive* or *acted upon,* receiving the effect of an action. *Passion,* as expressed by a verb, is simply the effect of an action, whether actual suffering or merely endurance or inaction.

A neuter verb may express simply *being;* as, He *is* wise. Or it may express a *state of being;* as, She *sleeps.*—He *sits*—It *stands.*

An active verb is either *transitive* or *intransitive.*

An **active-transitive verb** expresses an action which has some person or thing for its object; as, Cain *slew* Abel. —He *built* a house.

An **active-intransitive verb** expresses an action that has no person or thing for its object; as, John *walks.*—Fire *burns.*

Verbs are, therefore, divided, with respect to their signification, into four classes: **active-transitive, active-intransitive, passive,** and **neuter** verbs.

The word *neuter* means *neither;* that is, as applied to verbs, expressing neither action nor passion.

Both active and passive verbs express action, one as performed by the subject, the other as received by the subject. In the latter case, the object of the action becomes the subject of the verb.

Therefore, every active-transitive verb may be changed into a passive verb, and sometimes it is necessary to make this change. The following are examples:—

Active Verbs.	Passive Verbs.
Cain *slew* Abel.	Abel *was slain* by Cain.
John *wrote* the letter.	The letter *was written* by John.
He *killed* the bird.	The bird *was killed* by him.

Active-transitive and passive verbs are thus closely related. On this account some treat the passive verb as a form of the active-transitive, the latter being called the **active voice,** and the other the **passive voice.**

Exercises.

1. *Parse each of the verbs in the following sentences.*

1. He won the wager. 2. The boat moves rapidly. 3. The kite rose swiftly. 4. The river is frozen. 5. He sleeps too long. 6. The book lay on the desk. 7. Charles was punished. 8. She was afraid. 9. He was frightened. 10. You should obey your parents. 11. The dog howled. 12. The cat caught a mouse. 13. She sat at the piano. 14. The man stood motionless.

2. *Construct another sentence from each of the verbs in the above, changing every active-transitive verb into a passive verb.*

LESSON LIX.

MODIFICATIONS OF VERBS.—MOODS.

The different *manner* in which the being or action may be expressed by the verb causes a modification called *moods.*

Mood, or *mode,* means *manner.*

1. When the action or being is simply declared, or indicated, the verb is said to be in the **indicative mood ;** as, I *write.*—I *am speaking.*

2. When the power, liberty, possibility, or necessity of the being or action is expressed, the verb is said to be in the **potential mood;** as, I *may write.*—I *can write.*—I *must write.*

3. When the being or action is expressed as a supposition, a contingent or uncertain event in the future, or as the condition upon which some other event is to happen, the verb is said to be in the **subjunctive mood.**

The following afford illustrations:—
1. I will pardon him, if he *repent.*
2. I will go to-morrow, unless it *rain.*
3. I will reward him, if he *do* right.

In all these cases the verb is used in a *subjoined*, or added, clause; and, therefore, this has been called the *subjunctive mood.*

There may, however, be a subjoined clause without requiring the subjunctive mood. This is the case when the event is neither uncertain nor future, as in the following examples:—
1. He does not murmur, though he *is* suffering.
2. I intend to go, even if it *does rain.*

The subjunctive mood cannot be used without the subjoined clause.

4. When the being or action is expressed as a command, a request, or an entreaty, the verb is said to be in the **imperative mood;** as, *Go* immediately.—*Forgive* me.—*Be* comforted.

5. When the being or action is expressed without being limited or modified by any particular subject, the verb is said to be in the **infinitive mood;** as, To *be.*—To *do.*—To *suffer.*

In this mood, the word *to* usually precedes the verb.

A verb in any other mood, and limited by a subject, is called a **finite verb.**

Questions may be asked in either the indicative or potential mood.

Exercises.

1. *Copy the verbs in the following sentences, and write after each the mood in which it is found, giving the reason why it is in that mood.*

1. He is sick. 2. I went away. 3. He may go to Europe. 4. You can go home. 5. Did he write? 6. Must I do it? 7. I am to go there. 8. To exercise is necessary. 9. What did he say? 10. Speak plainly. 11. I will see him, if he come. 12. I will go, unless it be too cold.

2. *Analyze by diagram the last two sentences, and prepare a written parsing exercise of the words in each.*

LESSON LX.

DEFINITIONS OF THE MOODS.—REVIEW.

Moods are different forms of the verb, each of which expresses the being or action in some particular manner.

Action, in all these definitions, refers to that expressed not only by the active but the passive verb. The latter is sometimes called *passion*, because it is the endurance of the effect of action. (See *Lesson* LVIII.)

There are five moods: the **infinitive,** the **indicative,** the **potential,** the **subjunctive,** and the **imperative.**

The **infinitive mood** is that form of the verb which expresses the being or action in an unlimited manner.

The **indicative mood** is that form of the verb which simply indicates or declares a thing.

The **potential mood** is that form of the verb which expresses the power, liberty, possibility, or necessity of the being or action.

The **subjunctive mood** is that form of the verb which represents the being or action as conditional, doubtful, and contingent.

The **imperative mood** is that form of the verb which is used in commanding, exhorting, entreating, or permitting.

Questions for Review.

What is a compound relative pronoun? What words are compound relatives? What simple word is used as a compound relative? To what word is it equivalent? How may a verb represent the subject? How are verbs divided in respect to their signification? What is an active-transitive verb? An active-intransitive verb? A passive verb? A neuter verb? What is a finite verb?

LESSON LXI.

FORMS OF THE MOODS.

Moods are expressed by variations in the form of the verb, or by additional words.

_{The verb, in the English language, has very few variations in form, or inflections.}

The **indicative mood** is mostly expressed by the common form of the verb; as, I *speak.*—He *spoke.*

The **potential mood** is expressed by the word *may*, implying liberty or possibility; *can,* implying power; or *must*, implying necessity.

The **subjunctive mood** varies but slightly in form from the indicative.

The **infinitive** and **imperative moods** have mostly the common form of the verb.

Words such as *may, can,* and *must,* which are used to ex-

FORMS OF THE MOODS.

press the modifications of verbs, are called **auxiliary verbs** (that is, *helping verbs*).

Exercise.

Write in diagram form the sentences below. Give the oral analysis of each, stating whether simple, compound, or complex, and parse the words, classifying the verbs, and stating the mood of each.

MODEL.

How can he do it, unless his brother help him?

ORAL ANALYSIS.—A compound sentence, because it consists of two independent clauses connected by the conjunction *unless*. [Analyze each clause.]

PARSING OF THE VERBS.—*Can do* is an active-transitive verb, having for its object the pronoun *it*. It is in the potential mood, because it expresses power.

Help is an active-transitive verb, having for its object the pronoun *him*. It is in the subjunctive mood, being in the subjoined clause, and expressing uncertainty.

1. I did not see the error until it was pointed out.
2. Do not undertake the task if it be beyond your ability.
3. I shall come, unless something occur to prevent me.
4. He was not able to write to his friend yesterday.
5. You may have the book which you desire.
6. I cannot go, if the vessel sail to-morrow.
7. They who would succeed must exert themselves.

1. Contains an adverbial clause. See *Lesson* LIII.
2. *Beyond your ability* is a prepositional phrase, used as an adjective attribute.
4. *To write to his friend yesterday* is an adjunct of *able*. It is a complex phrase; the principal part, is *write*.
6. The verb *sail* is in the subjunctive mood, because it is uncertain whether the vessel will sail or not. If it were certain, the verb would be in the indicative mood, and the form would be *sails*.

LESSON LXII.

TENSES.

Tenses are modifications of the verb that distinguish time.

In the use of the verb in this regard, we are to express:—
1. That the time of the being or action is present, past, or future; as, I *love.*—I *loved.*—I *shall love.*
2. That the being or action is *completed* in present, past, or future time; as, I *have loved.*—I *had loved.*—I *shall have loved.*

Hence there must be *six tenses* to express this twofold distinction.

The following illustrates this:—

Distinctions.		Names of Tenses.
1. Present	Imperfect	Present.
2. Past	or	Imperfect, or Past.
3. Future	Indefinite	First Future.
4. Present		Perfect, or Present Perfect.
5. Past	Perfect	Pluperfect, or Past Perfect.
6. Future		Second Future, or Future Perfect.

DEFINITIONS.

There are six tenses: the **present**, the **imperfect**, the **perfect**, the **pluperfect**, the **first future**, and the **second future.**

The **present tense** is that which expresses what now *exists*, or *is taking* place; as, I *hear* a noise; somebody *is coming.*

The **imperfect tense** is that which expresses what *took* place, or *was occurring*, in time fully past; as, I *saw* him yesterday; he *was walking* out.

The **perfect tense** is that which expresses what *has taken* place, within some period of time not yet fully past; as, I *have seen* him to-day.

The **pluperfect tense** is that which expresses what *had taken* place, at some past time mentioned; as, I *had seen* him, when I met you.

The **first-future tense** is that which expresses what *will take* place hereafter; as, I *shall see* him again.

The **second-future tense** is that which expresses what *will have taken* place, at some future time mentioned; as, I *shall have seen* him by to-morrow noon.

Exercises.

1. *Write the mood and tense of every verb in the following sentences.*

1. I shall go home. 2. You must stay here. 3. He went away. 4. He can do it. 5. Tell me the story. 6. I saw him yesterday. 7. I have seen him to-day. 8. I had written the letter when you called. 9. What will you do? 10. Whom shall I call? 11. Bring [to] me your slate. 12. He will have finished the work by to-morrow. 13. It will have been finished by next week. 14. If this be the truth, it will sorely grieve your kind mother.

2. *Analyze by diagram Sentences* 8, 12, *and* 14.

LESSON LXIII.

FORMS OF THE TENSES.

The indicative mood has six tenses, formed chiefly by means of the auxiliary verbs *do* (imperfect, *did*), *have* (imperfect, *had*), *shall*, and *will*.

The forms of the verb *love* in the indicative mood, arranged in the order of the tenses, and as used with a subject of the first person, singular number, are here given.

TENSE FORMS OF THE VERB **LOVE,** INDICATIVE MOOD.

I *love* or *do love;* I *loved* or *did love;* I *have loved;* I *had loved;* I *shall love;* I *shall have loved.*

The second of the two forms of the present and imperfect tenses is used for emphasis, and in interrogation; as, I *do* love. —Do I love?

The potential mood has four tenses. These are formed by the use of the auxiliary verbs *may* (imperfect, *might*), *can* (imperfect, *could*), *must*, *would* (imperfect of *will*), and *should* (imperfect of *shall*).

The present, imperfect, perfect, and pluperfect tenses of the potential mood of the verb *love*, in the first person singular, are:

TENSE FORMS OF THE VERB **LOVE,** POTENTIAL MOOD.

I *may, can,* or *must love;* I *might, could, would,* or *should love;* I *may, can,* or *must have loved;* I *might, could, would,* or *should have loved.*

The subjunctive mood has two tenses, the present and imperfect, which are the same or nearly the same as those of the indicative; as, If I *love;* If I *loved.*

The imperative mood has one tense, the present, which is the simple form of the verb. It is used with a subject of the second person; as, *Love* (thou or you), or *Do* you *love.*

The infinitive mood has two tenses, the present and the perfect; as, To *love,* to *have loved.*

Exercise.

Write the forms of the tenses of the following verbs in each mood, with the pronoun I, except in the infinitive mood.

Walk. Parse. Learn. Work. Read. Write.

LESSON LXIV.
TENSE FORMS OF THE VERB "BE."

The following synopsis contains all the forms of the verb *be*, as used with the subject *I*, of the first person, singular number.

Infinitive.—To be, to have been.
Indicative.—I am, I was, I have been, I had been, I shall be, I shall have been.
Potential.—I may, can, *or* must be; I might, could, would, *or* should be; I may, can, *or* must have been; I might, could, would, *or* should have been.
Subjunctive.—(If) I be, (if) I were.
Imperative.—Be (thou) *or*, Do (thou) be.
The imperative mood is used only with a subject of the second person.

Exercises.

1. *In the same manner, write a synopsis of the verbs* do, speak, give, *and* think.
2. *Write six sentences containing examples of the six tenses of the indicative mood with the subject* I.

Questions for Review.

How are moods expressed? How is the indicative mood expressed? The potential mood? The subjunctive mood? The infinitive and imperative moods? For what are auxiliary verbs used? What are tenses? How many tenses are there? Why must there be six tenses? Name the tenses. What is the present tense? The imperfect tense? The perfect tense? The pluperfect tense? The first-future tense? The second-future tense? How many tenses has the indicative mood? How many has the potential mood? How many has the subjunctive mood? The imperative mood? The infinitive mood? What are the forms of the tenses in the indicative, with a subject of the first person, singular number? Of the potential mood? Of the subjunctive mood? What are the forms of the tenses of each mood of the verb *be*, for the first person, singular number?

LESSON LXV.

PARTICIPLES.

Connected with the verb and its forms are the **participles.**

It is especially necessary to know the forms of the participles, as some of the tenses are formed from them. Examples are here given from the verbs *love* and *write*.

Love.

	Active.	*Passive.*
Imperfect.	Loving.	Being loved.
Perfect.	Loved.	Loved.
Preperfect.	Having loved.	Having been loved.

Write.

	Active.	*Passive.*
Imperfect.	Writing.	Being written.
Perfect.	Written.	Written.
Preperfect.	Having written.	Having been written.

A verb has three participles: the **imperfect,** the **perfect,** and the **preperfect.**

The **imperfect participle** implies a continuance of the being or action.

The **perfect participle** implies a completion of the being or action.

The **preperfect participle** implies a completion of the being or action previous to some other past event; as, "*Having finished* my task, I went home."

The imperfect participle of all active verbs is formed by adding *ing* to the present infinitive; as, *loving, working, being.*

The perfect participle of all *regular verbs* is formed by adding *d* or *ed* to the present infinitive.

The preperfect participle is always formed by prefixing having to the perfect participle; as, *having seen, having written.*

A phrase beginning with a participle is called a **participial phrase.**

Exercises.

Analyze in diagram form the following sentences. Write a list of the participles, putting to the right of each the class to which it belongs.

MODEL.

Having received a serious injury, he was confined to his bed for a long time.

```
        He  ------------------  was confined
                                   | to      | for
      having received ---| injury  | bed     | time
                     a  |          |  a
                 serious|       his| long
```

The relation of the participle and its object is indicated in this diagram by the single dotted line.

1. Being afraid, I could not make so great a venture.
2. Loving his parents fondly, he would not treat them disrespectfully.
3. Playing at ball, he met with a very serious accident.
4. Having returned from the country, he resumed his work.
5. Being disturbed at the news, he immediately returned home.
6. He stood dismayed at the sight of so much suffering.

LESSON LXVI.

REGULAR AND IRREGULAR VERBS.

A complete verb has four **principal parts:** the **present** (infinitive), the **preterit** (imperfect indicative), the **imperfect participle,** and the **perfect participle.**

There are a few verbs that want some of these parts, and are therefore called **defective verbs.**

A **regular verb** is one that forms its preterit and perfect participle by assuming *d* or *ed;* as, *love, loved, loved.*

An **irregular verb** is one that does not form its preterit and perfect participle by assuming *d* or *ed;* as, *think, thought, thought; see, saw, seen.*

Verbs that have both regular and irregular forms are called *redundant verbs;* as, *dress, dressed, dressed,* or, *dress, drest, drest.*

As the imperfect participle is always formed the same way, we need to know only the preterit and perfect participle of a verb to be able to form all its tenses.

For a complete list of irregular and redundant verbs, see APPENDIX.

SYNOPSIS OF THE MOODS AND TENSES OF THE VERB **See.**

Principal Parts.—*Pres.*, See ; *Pret.*, Saw ; *Perf. Part.*, Seen.

Indicative Mood.—I see, I saw, I have seen, I had seen, I shall see, I shall have seen.

Potential Mood.—I may, can, *or* must see ; I might, could, would, *or* should see ; I may, can, *or* must have seen ; I might, could, would, *or* should have seen.

Subjunctive Mood.—(If) I see, (if) I saw.

Imperative Mood.—See (thou or you). (2d Pers. Sing.)

Exercise.

Write a similar synopsis for the following verbs, the principal parts of which are given.

1. Blow, blew, blown.
2. Strive, strove, striven.
3. Fight, fought, fought.
4. Give, gave, given.
5. Sit, sat, sat.
6. Set, set, set.
7. Lie, lay, lain.
8. Lay, laid, laid.

LESSON LXVII.

PERSON AND NUMBER OF VERBS.

The **person** and **number** of verbs are those modifications which depend on the person and number of the subject.

The modifications, or inflections, for this purpose are very few. Those proper to the first person, singular, have already been given. The second person, singular, requires the ending *st* or *est* in the form of the verb itself, or in that of the auxiliary; except in the sujunctive mood.

Shall and *will*, however, are changed to *shalt* and *wilt*. Moreover, *will* in the second and third persons expresses the the same as *shall* in the first person, namely, simply a future event; while *will* in the first person, and *shall* in the second and third person, imply the exercise of will or determination on the part of the speaker or writer.

The forms of all three persons, in the plural number, are the same as those of the first person, singular.

SYNOPSIS OF **Love** (Second Person, Singular).

Indicative.—Thou lovest *or* dost love, lovedst *or* didst love, hast loved, hadst loved, shalt *or* wilt love, shalt *or* wilt have loved.

Potential.—Thou mayst, canst, *or* must love; mightst, couldst, wouldst, *or* shouldst love; mayst, canst, or must have loved; mightst, couldst, wouldst, *or* shouldst have loved.

Subjunctive.—(If) thou love, (if) thou loved. The third person, singular, in the present tense, indicative mood, adds *s* to to the verb; as, He *loves*, he *sees*, he *thinks*, he *does*.

The third person singular, in solemn style, often has the ending *th* instead of *s*; as, he *loveth*, he *goeth*, he *hath*, he *doth*.

In the verb *have*, the regular forms of the second and third persons, singular, are contracted into *hast* and *has;* as, I *have*, thou *hast*, he *has* (instead of *havest* and *haves*).

Exercise.

Write a synopsis of the tenses of the following verbs, in the person and number specified.

1. Begin, began, begun. (First person, singular.)
2. Choose, chose, chosen. (Second person, singular.)
3. Do, did, done. (Third person, singular.)
4. Fall, fell, fallen. (First person, plural.)
5. Flee, fled, fled. (Second person, plural.)
6. Fly, flew, flown. (Third person, plural.)

LESSON LXVIII.

THE CONJUGATION OF VERBS.

The **conjugation** of a verb is a regular arrangement of its moods, tenses, persons, numbers, and participles.

The following is an example.

Conjugation of the Verb BE.
Principal Parts.

Present.	*Preterit.*	*Imperfect Participle.*	*Perfect Participle.*
Be.	Was.	Being.	Been.

INFINITIVE MOOD.

Present Tense. To be.
Perfect Tense. To have been.

INDICATIVE MOOD.
Present Tense.

Singular.	*Plural.*
1. I am,	1. We are,
2. Thou art,	2. You are,
3. He is;	3. They are.

THE CONJUGATION OF VERBS.

Imperfect Tense.

Singular.
1. I was,
2. Thou wast,
3. He was,

Plural.
1. We were,
2. You were,
3. They were.

Perfect Tense.

Singular.
1. I have been,
2. Thou hast been,
3. He has been;

Plural.
1. We have been,
2. You have been,
3. They have been.

Pluperfect Tense.

Singular.
1. I had been,
2. Thou hadst been,
3. He had been;

Plural.
1. We had been,
2. You had been,
3. They had been.

First-future Tense.

Singular.
1. I shall be,
2. Thou wilt be,
3. He will be;

Plural.
1. We shall be,
2. You will be,
3. They will be.

Second-future Tense.

Singular.
1. I shall have been,
2. Thou wilt have been,
3. He will have been;

Plural.
1. We shall have been,
2. You will have been,
3. They will have been.

POTENTIAL MOOD.

Present Tense.

Singular.
1. I may be,
2. Thou mayst be,
3. He may be;

Plural.
1. We may be,
2. You may be,
3. They may be.

Imperfect Tense.

Singular.
1. I might be,
2. Thou mightst be,
3. He might be;

Plural.
1. We might be,
2. You might be,
3. They might be.

Perfect Tense.

Singular.	*Plural.*
1. I may have been,	1. We may have been,
2. Thou mayst have been,	2. You may have been,
3. He may have been;	3. They may have been.

Pluperfect Tense.

Singular.	*Plural.*
1. I might have been,	1. We might have been,
2. Thou mightst have been,	2. You might have been,
3. He might have been;	3. They might have been.

SUBJUNCTIVE MOOD.

Present Tense.

Singular.	*Plural.*
1. If I be,	1. If we be,
2. If thou be,	2. If you be,
3. If he be;	3. If they be.

Imperfect Tense.

Singular.	*Plural.*
1. If I were,	1. If we were,
2. If thou wert, *or* were,	2. If you were,
3. If he were;	3. If they were.

IMPERATIVE MOOD.

Present Tense.

Singular. 2. Be [thou] *or* Do thou be.
Plural. 2. Be [ye *or* you,] *or* Do you be.

PARTICIPLES.

1. *The Imperfect.*   2. *The Perfect.*   3. *The Preperfect.*
   Being.   Been.   Having been.

The chief irregularities of this verb, it will be seen, are in the present and imperfect tenses of the indicative mood—in the forms

COMPOUND CONJUGATIONS.

am, are, art, was, and *were.* The other tenses are formed in the general way from the perfect participle *been.*

Exercise.

Write out the conjugation of the verbs **love, have, do,** and **fly.**

LESSON LXIX.

COMPOUND CONJUGATIONS.

Active and neuter verbs may also be conjugated by adding the imperfect participle to the verb *be*, through all its changes.

This is the *compound form* of conjugation, and, as it implies a continuance of the action or state of being, it is sometimes called the **progressive form.**

The synopsis of the first person, singular, indicative mood, of the verb *write* is here given as an example.

I *am writing,* I *was writing,* I *have been writing,* I *had been writing,* I *shall be writing,* I *shall have been writing.*

[The pupil should be required to write the synopsis of the other moods.]

Passive verbs are always compound, being formed from active-transitive verbs by adding the perfect participle to the verb *be* through all its changes.

Synopsis of the Passive Verb BE LOVED.

Infinitive. Present, To *be loved;* perfect to *have been loved.*

Indicative. I *am loved, was loved, have been loved, had been loved, shall be loved, shall have been loved.*

Potential. I *may be loved, might be loved, may have been loved, might have been loved.*

Subjunctive. (If) I *be loved*, (if) I *were loved*.
Imperative. *Be loved* (thou or you), or *Do* (thou or you) *be loved*.

Exercise.

Write out the conjugation of the active verb **Be writing**. Also of the passive verb **Be taught**.

LESSON LXX.

AUXILIARY AND DEFECTIVE VERBS.

An **auxiliary** is a short verb prefixed to one of the principal parts of another verb, to express some particular mode and time of the being or action.

The auxiliaries are *do, be, have, shall, will, may, can,* and *must*, with their variations.

All the auxiliaries except *do, be,* and *have* are defective verbs. *Do, be,* and *have* are also used as principal verbs.

The defective verbs are used only in the present and imperfect tenses of the indicative mood; as, *can, could; may, might; must, must; shall, should; will, would.*

Ought and a few other verbs, rarely used, are also defective verbs.

A **defective verb** is a verb that wants some of the principal parts.

When any of the principal parts are wanting, the tenses usually derived from those parts are, of course, also wanting.

Exercises.

1. *Analyze in diagram form the following sentences.*
2. *Write the parsing of the separate words.*

1. He might have succeeded, if he had tried hard enough.
2. He will have finished the letter before you call.

THE USE OF WOULD AND SHOULD. 107

3. What has been done cannot be repaired.
4. The horse must be shod, or he will become lame.
5. You shall do it, for I will compel you.
6. I shall be glad to see you when you call.
7. You will perform the task well, for I shall help you.

EXAMPLE.—" I shall be glad to see you when you call."

DIAGRAM.

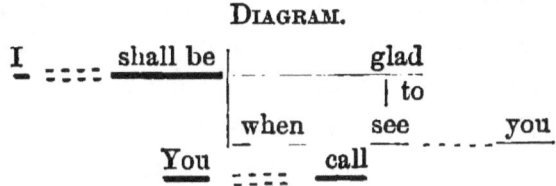

FORM OF A WRITTEN PARSING EXERCISE.

Word.	Part of Speech.	Class.	Modification.	Relation.
I	Pronoun.	Personal.	1st, Sing., Com., Nom.	Subj. of Shall be.
Shall Be	Verb.	Irregular, Neuter.	Indic., 1st Fut., 1st, Sing.	Pred. Verb.
Glad	Adjective.	Common.	Positive degree.	Att.
To	Preposition.			Bet. *glad* and *see*.
See	Verb.	Irregular Act. Trans.	Infin., Pres.	Obj. of *to*.
You	Pronoun.	Personal.	2d, pl., Com., Obj.	Obj. of *see*.
When	Adverb.	Of time.		Adj't of *call*.
You	Pronoun.	Personal.	2d, pl., Com., Nom.	Subj. of *call*.
Call.	Verb.	Regular Act. Int.	Indic., Pres., 2d pl.	Pred. Verb.

LESSON LXXI.

THE USE OF WOULD AND SHOULD.

The preterits **would** and **should** require the same discrimination as **will** and **shall**. (See *Lesson* LXVII.)

Shall and **should,** when used in the first person, imply only a future event; as, I *shall* go to-morrow.—We *should* go, if it were possible.

Will and **would,** when used in the second or third person, imply only a future event; as, You *will* go to-morrow. — They *would* write, if they could.

Shall and **should,** when used in the second or third person, imply the exercise of will on the part of the speaker or writer; as, You *shall* do it; i. e., *I am resolved to make you do it.*—You should do it, if I could make you; i. e., *I would compel you.* Should is often equivalent to *ought.*

Will and **would,** when used in the first person, imply the exercise of will or determination on the part of the speaker or writer; as, I *will* go; i. e., *I am resolved to go.* —I *would* do it, if I could; i. e., *I should be willing to do it.*

Do not use *will* or *would* in connection with words that imply will or inclination.

Thus say, *I should like to do it,* not *I would like; I should be pleased,* not *I would be pleased; I shall be glad,* not *I will be glad.* We do not *will* to be willing, to be pleased, or to be glad.

Exercise.

Analyze the following sentences in diagram form.
Explain the use of shall and will, and should and would.

1. I shall fail, unless my brother will help me.
2. It will certainly be a very great misfortune for him.
3. I should be much pleased to learn of your success.
4. Will you attend the meeting of the board to-morrow?
5. They should be entirely willing to make that sacrifice.
6. I would not, under any circumstances, do what he requests.
7. My sister would be pleased to oblige you, if it were possible.

LESSON LXXII.

ADVERBS.—CLASSES.

There are four classes of adverbs; namely, adverbs of **time,** of **place,** of **degree,** and of **manner;** besides others that modify the predicate in various ways.

Adverbs of time are those which answer to the question, *When? How long? How soon? How often?*

As, *now, already, hereafter, when, then, ever, often, first, secondly,* etc.

Adverbs of place are those which answer to the question, *Where,* or *in what place? Whither,* or *to what place? Whence,* or *from what place?*

As, *where, there, here; whither, thither, hither; whence, thence, hence; somewhere.*

Adverbs of degree are those which answer to the question, *How much? How little?*

As, *much, enough, little, somewhat, so, as, very, equally, ever so, scarcely, hardly, how.*

Adverbs of manner are those which answer to the question, *How,* or *in what manner?*

As, *well, ill, thus, so, like, foolishly, wisely, justly, skillfully.*

Some words are often placed in the general class of adverbs of manner, although they do not express the manner of the being or action, but serve to modify the predicate, or show the *manner of the predication.* The following are examples:—

1. Affirmation; as, *verily, truly, indeed, surely,* etc.
2. Negation; as, *not, nowise.*
3. Doubt; as, *perhaps, possibly, perchance.*
4. Cause; as, *why, wherefore, therefore.*

A **conjunctive adverb** is one that connects different clauses of a sentence.

Adverbs are sometimes compared like adjectives: some regularly; as, *soon, sooner, soonest; often, oftener, oftenest;* others irregularly; as, *well, better, best; badly* or *ill, worse, worst; little, less, least; much, more, most; far, farther, farthest; forth, further, furthest.*

Exercises in Construction.

1. *Write three sentences, each containing an adverb of* **manner.**
2. "   "   "   "   "   "   "   " **place.**
3. "   "   "   "   "   "   "   " **time.**
4. "   "   "   "   "   "   "   " **degree.**
5. *Write sentences, each containing one of the following adverbs:—*

Sufficiently, secondly, perhaps, truly, why, hereafter, always.

LESSON LXXIII.

CONJUNCTIONS.

Conjunctions are divided into two general classes, **copulative** and **disjunctive** conjunctions.

A **copulative conjunction** is one that denotes an addition, a cause, or a supposition.

A **disjunctive conjunction** is one that denotes opposition of meaning.

The principal copulative conjunctions are *and, as, both, because, for, if, that.*

The principal disjunctive conjunctions are *or, nor, either, neither, than, though, although, yet, but, except, whether, lest, unless, save, notwithstanding.*

These words conjoin, or connect, in construction, while they express a contrast or opposition in the sense, or meaning. Hence the term *disjunctive*.

Conjunctions used in pairs are called **corresponsive conjunctions.**

The following are examples: *Both—and, as—as, as—so, if— then, either—or, neither—nor, whether—or, though—yet.*

Corresponsive conjunctions serve to make the connection of words, phrases, or clauses more forcible or emphatic.

The following are *conjunctive phrases;* that is, phrases used as simple conjunctions: *as though, inasmuch as, in order that, so that, as well as,* etc.

Examples.

1. Both William and Henry are deserving of blame.
2. Neither the fear of punishment nor the hope of reward could keep him from doing wrong.
3. Though you should lose your life, you should persevere in doing your duty.
4. Whether he succeed or fail in the undertaking, he will gain applause.
5. I will meet you either in the morning or in the afternoon.

Exercise.

Analyze by diagram the above sentences, and parse the separate words.

Model.

Though I should be wholly abandoned by my friends, yet will I not be utterly cast down.

```
         |  I  ......... should be | abandoned   |
         |         wholly  |       by            |
Though   |                         | friends     | yet
         |                    my   |             |
         |  I  .... will | be cast down          |
         |                 not          utterly  |
```

This diagram shows the double connection of the two clauses.

Are these clauses dependent or independent?
They are independent.

Why?
Because they are merely connected, without any grammatical dependence. Neither of them is used as an adjunct.

LESSON LXXIV.
PREPOSITIONS.

Prepositions are neither principal parts of a sentence nor adjuncts, their office being only to express *relation*.

Prepositions introduce phrases that are generally used as adjuncts.

The preposition always expresses the relation between its object and the word of which the phrase is an adjunct, or to which the phrase relates.

For example, in the sentence, "The invention was *of no use*," the phrase *of no use*, equivalent to the adjective *useless*, is an attribute, relating to the subject noun *invention;* and, therefore, the preposition expresses the relation between the nouns *invention* and *use*. It was an *invention of no use*, or a *useless invention*.

While we speak of a preposition as expressing the relation of one *word* to another, it must be borne in mind that, properly speaking, it is the relation between the *things*, or *ideas*, denoted by the words that is expressed by the preposition.

The following list contains the chief simple prepositions:—

Aboard, about, above, across, after, against, along, amid or *amidst, among* or *amongst, around, at, athwart ;—before, behind, below, beneath, beside* or *besides, between* or *betwixt, beyond, by ;— concerning ;—down, during ;—except, excepting ;—for, from ;—in, into ;—notwithstanding ;—of, off, on, over, over-thwart —past ;— round ;—since ;—through, throughout, till, to, touching, toward* or *towards; under, underneath, until, unto, up, upon ;—with, within, without.*

USE OF PREPOSITIONS.

Two or more words are sometimes used as a **compound preposition,** being so combined as to express a single relation ; as, *according to, because of, out of, as to, as for, from out, from among,* from between, *over against.*

Prepositions, when used without any object, become adverbs; as, "He walked *about.*"—"It went *up.*"—"It came *down* rapidly."

Prepositions, when used merely for connection, become conjunctions. Thus *for,* when it means *because,* and *except,* when it means *unless,* are conjunctions; as, "I was shivering, *for* it was cold."—"*Except* ye remain in the ship, ye cannot be saved."

Exercises.

1. *Insert the required prepositions in each of the following sentences.*

1. They marched ―― the enemy ―― the break ―― day. 2. Live ―― peace ―― all. 3. Do not go ―― the bounds ―― propriety. 4. Keep ―― the limits ―― truth and rectitude. 5. The book lay ―― him ―― the desk. 6. Act kindly ―― all. 7. He found himself ―― two fires. 8. The squirrel ran ―― the tree, and ―― the branches, jumping ―― one ―― the other ―― great rapidity.

2. *Make a list of the prepositions in these sentences, and write the terms of relation of each.*

LESSON LXXV.

USE OF PREPOSITIONS.

Care should be taken to use the proper preposition, in order to express correctly the relation of the terms, according to general usage.

The following prepositions are to be carefully distinguished.

1. { **Below.**—He looked *below* the place on which he stood.
   { **Beneath.**—I descended into the mine far *beneath* the surface.
2. { **Among.** He divided it *among* the company.
   { **Between.**—*Between* the two brothers there was a quarrel.

3. { **By.**—Samuel was struck *by* his cousin.
{ **With.**—He cut the apple *with* his knife.

4. { **On.**—They were all lying *on* the ground.
{ **Upon.**—She put her book *upon* the shelf.

5. { **Of.**—They met within a mile *of* the town.
{ **From.**—He went about two miles *from* the place.

6. { **In.**—He was taking a walk *in* the garden.
{ **Into.**—I opened the gate and walked *into* the garden.

7. { **Over.**—In his address, he went *over* the whole ground.
{ **Under.** { The deed was given *under* his hand and seal.
{ The letter was written *under* his own signature.

Explanations.

1. *Beneath* is farther down than *below*.

2. *Between* is used with reference to *two* only; *among*, to *three* or *more*.

3. *By* denotes the agent or doer; *with*, the instrument or means.

4. *On* with its object denotes a place or situation; *upon*, a movement upward to the place.

5. *Of* when used in this way, implies measurement from; *from*, direction of movement, being the reverse of *toward*. Thus we say *to* and *fro* (*toward* and *from*).

6. *In* implies rest or movement within a place; *into*, movement from without to within.

7. *Over* is *above; under*, at the lower side or surface. The paper receiving the signature or seal is *under the hand*.

Exercises.

1. *Write a sentence to illustrate the use of each of the above prepositions.*

2. *Insert the proper preposition in each of the blanks in the following sentences.*

   1. There was a strife —— the two brothers.
   2. They hid themselves —— the trees.
   3. John was accidentally injured —— his brother —— a gun.
   4. He was lying —— the ground, —— a tree.
   5. I put the book —— a shelf —— the closet.

PARTICIPIAL PHRASES.

6. Charles was standing ——— the boat, and fell ——— the river.
7. He made the statement ——— his own signature.
8. I looked ——— me, and saw a deep cavern far ——— the surface of the earth.
9. The house had a deep cellar ——— the ground floor.
10. He said it was ——— his dignity to do what he was asked to do.

LESSON LXXVI.

PARTICIPIAL PHRASES.

Participial phrases, like participles, are used both as adjectives and as nouns.

The following sentences contain examples :—

First Class (*Adjectives*).

1. I saw him *coming across the street.* - - -
2. Truth *crushed to earth* shall rise again.
3. The letter, *being written hastily*, is faulty.
4. *Having completed his work*, he demanded payment.
5. *Having been punished for his fault*, he soon gave proof of repentance.

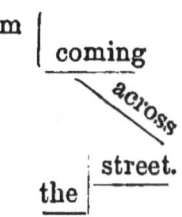

Second Class (*Nouns*).

6. Charles is fond of *studying* history.
7. Before *undertaking* the work he prepared himself.
8. After *having been rewarded*, he went away.
9. *Hunting* the buffalo is exciting sport.
10. *Giving* alms indiscriminately is not a wise practice.

Participial phrases, when used as nouns, are sometimes preceded by a noun or pronoun in the possessive case.

The following are examples:—
11. There is no use in John's denying his guilt.
12. I am surprised at your making that statement.
13. On our arriving at the house, there was great excitement.
14. On arriving at the house we found great excitement.

In Sentence 13, *our* is required to show what the participle refers to. If it were omitted, the participle would, grammatically, relate to excitement. In Sentence 14, the possessive pronoun is not needed, as the participle properly relates to *we*.

Exercises.

1. *Analyze by diagram the above sentences and analyze them orally.*
2. *Write a parsing exercise from Sentences* 1, 2, 5, 6, 9, 11.

MODELS.

1. "Hunting the wild deer in the woods affords great pleasure to some persons."

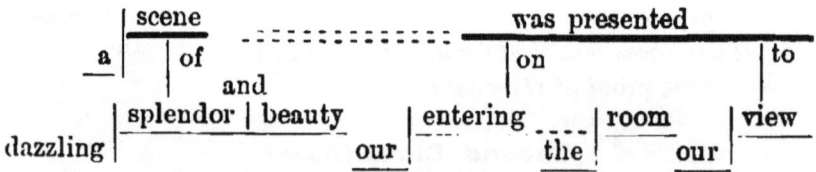

2. "On our entering the room, a scene of dazzling splendor and beauty was presented to our view."

3. *Write two or more sentences, each containing a participial phrase used as an adjective.*
4. *Write two or more sentences, each containing a participial phrase used as a noun.*

PUNCTUATION.—Participial phrases placed out of their natural order (as in 4 and 5), or not used as modifying adjuncts, should be separated by a comma.

LESSON LXXVII.

USE OF THE INFINITIVE MOOD.

The **infinitive mood** is generally preceded by the word *to*, which usually serves to express the relation between the infinitive verb and some other word in the sentence, thus performing the office of a preposition.

The following are examples:
1. She has a *desire to learn*.
2. He was *careful to avoid* danger.
3. He exerted himself *sufficiently to succeed*.
4. He *came* here *to explain* the matter.

In 1, *to* is a preposition, and expresses the relation between the infinitive *learn* and the noun *desire*. In 2, it expresses the relation between *avoid* and the adjective *careful;* in 3, between *succeed* and the adverb *sufficiently;* in 4, between *explain* and the finite verb *came*.

In each of these cases the infinitive is, like a noun, the object of the preposition *to*.

The infinitive may be used in many other ways:
1. As the subject of a verb; as, "*To lie* is base."
2. As the object of a verb; as, "He loves *to study*."
3. As the adjective attribute; as, "He was *to blame*," or *to be blamed*, that is, *blamable*.
4. As a noun attribute; as, "To enjoy is *to obey*."

In examples 1, 2, and 4, the word *to* does not perform the office of a preposition, being used merely to denote the infinitive mood.

Exercises.

Analyze by diagram, and give the oral analysis of, the following sentences. Parse all the infinitives.

USE OF THE INFINITIVE MOOD.

MODELS.

1. "Exercising the greatest caution, this skilful navigator used every possible means to avoid the coming danger."

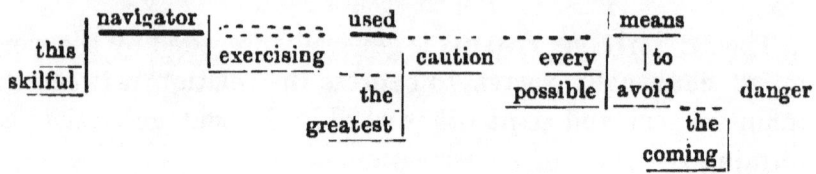

Every object is preceded by a dotted line, connecting it with the verb or participle on which it depends.

2. "To bestow alms without prudence is to give encouragement to idleness and beggary."

```
To bestow     alms   ____  is  _____  to give  _____  encouragement
   without                                 | to
 prudence                                  |    and
                                        idleness | beggary
```

ORAL PARSING.

Avoid is a regular active-transitive verb, the principal parts of which are *avoid, avoided, avoided.* It is in the infinitive mood and present tense, and is the object of the preposition *to* which expresses its relation to *means;* the phrase *to avoid the coming danger* relating as an adjective to *means.*

Bestow is a regular active-transitive verb; the principal parts are *bestow, bestowed, bestowed.* It is in the infinitive mood, present tense, and, with the phrase of which it is the principal part, is the subject of the verb *is.*

Give is an irregular active-transitive verb; the principal parts are *give, gave, given.* It is in the infinitive mood, present tense, and with the phrase of which it is the principal part is the attribute after *is.*

1. His effort to save his friend's life caused the loss of his own.
2. Be good enough to tell me what you think of the affair.
3. You are very kind to invite me to your party.
4. To do good to every one is the duty of a Christian.
5. He was much to be blamed for the course which he took.
6. The ship was to sail in the morning, but was delayed for several hours.

LESSON LXXVIII.

THE INFINITIVE OBJECT CLAUSE.

1. *They wished that he would leave the place.*
2. *They wished him to leave the place.*

What clause is the object of the verb *wished* in Sentence 1?
What is the object of *wished* in Sentence 2?

The object is, *him to leave the place*, which is equivalent to the clause in Sentence 1.

It is perfectly clear that the object of wished is not the pronoun *him*, nor is it *to leave the place;* for they wished neither of these. In this case we have a pronoun in the objective case subject to a verb in the infinitive mood. A clause thus formed being itself an object is called an *infinitive object clause*.

An **infinitive object clause** is a clause in which the being or action is expressed by a verb in the infinitive mood, and the subject of it is a noun or pronoun in the objective case.

An infinitive object clause may be the object also of a preposition; as, "It was shameful for *him to betray his friend*."

Exercises.

1. *Analyze in diagram form the following:*

1. John would not go to school though his parents wished him to go.
2. William's father forbade him to keep company with bad boys.
3. The general commanded his officers to begin the attack.
4. They begged the judge to show mercy in sentencing the prisoner.
5. The evidence proved him to be guilty of the crime of which he was accused.

MODEL.

The king sent messengers to command them to leave the country.

```
      | king ──── sent ──── messengers
The ──|        ──── to
               command ──── them ──── to leave ──── | country.
                                                the |
```

In this use of the infinitive mood, *to* loses its prepositional character and becomes a part of the verbal form, denoting the infinitive.

2. *Change each infinitive clause to one with a finite verb.* Thus :—

The king sent messengers to command that they should leave the country.

LESSON LXXIX.

COMPOUND AND COMPLEX PHRASES.

Phrases may be **simple, compound,** or **complex.**

A **compound phrase** is one that consists of two or more phrases connected by a conjunction; as, "Leaping from his horse and drawing his sword."

A **complex phrase** is one that contains a phrase used as an adjunct of its principal part; as, "In the spring *of the year.*"

The **principal part of a phrase** is the word on which all the other parts of the phrase depend; as, "*By* the *bounty* of Heaven."—"*Watching* him with care."

A phrase, the principal part of which is a verb in the infinitive mood, is called an **infinitive phrase;** as, "*To be* happy."—"*To do* good to all."—"*To be* fond of study."

In a participial phrase the principal part is the participle which introduces it; as, "Truth *crushed to earth.*"—"A man *perishing in the snow.*"

Phrases perform the office of various parts of speech:—

1. A noun; as, "*To be good* is *to be happy.*" That is, *Goodness* is *happiness.*
2. An adjective; as, "A man *of ability.*"—"A person *to be esteemed.*" That is, An *able* man.—An *estimable* person.
3. An adverb; as, "I returned *on the following day.*"

Phrases may be used in various constructions:—

1. As a subject; as, "*To do good* is our duty."
2. As an attribute; as, "Our wisest course is *to obey our conscience.*" (Noun.)—"His conduct is *much to be admired.*" (Adjective.)
3. As an object; as, "Never attempt *to conceal a fault.*"
4. As an explanatory adjunct; as, "It is best *to tell the truth.*" That is, It—to tell the truth—is best, the phrase being used to explain the preceding pronoun.
5. A phrase may be independent; as, "*To be candid,* I acknowledge that I was wrong."—"*Night coming on,* I lost my way."

The second construction, in which a noun or a pronoun is used independently with a participle, is equivalent to a dependent or subordinate clause.

Thus, "*He being young,* they deceived him," is equivalent to, *As he was young, they deceived him.*

When the principal part of an independent phrase is a pronoun, it should have the form of the nominative case; as, "*I* being young, they deceived me."—"*He* failing, who can succeed?"

Exercise.

Analyze by diagram the following sentences; give the oral analysis, classifying the phrases, and explaining their use. Parse the separate words.

1. In the beginning of the next month, the general planned another campaign against the strongest city of the enemy.

122   COMPOUND AND COMPLEX PHRASES.

2. To be fully on your guard will generally prevent an attack of your enemies.

3. It is the part of wisdom to make use of every opportunity for self-improvement.

4. His conduct was greatly to be admired on an occasion of so much importance.

5. On all occasions and in every way he vigorously opposed the project.

6. The ship having foundered at sea, all on board of her perished.

7. They having been successful, many were anxious to follow their example.

Model.

"In the fall of the year, we took a journey to the western part of the country, with the design to discover the best way over the mountains."

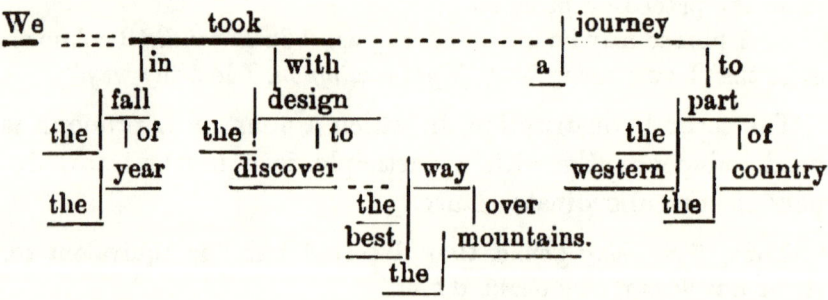

Oral Analysis.—This is a simple declarative sentence. The subject is *we*, and the predicate is the rest of the sentence. The predicate verb is *took*, and its adjuncts are the complex adverbial phrases, *in the fall of the year* and *with the design to discover the best way over the mountains*. The principal part of the first of these phrases is *fall*, and its adjuncts are *the* and the simple adjective phrase *of the year*. The principal part of the second phrase is *design*, and its adjuncts are *the* and the complex adjective phrase *to discover the best way over the mountains*. Of the latter phrase the principal part is *discover*, the object of which is *way;* and the adjuncts of *way* are *the*, *best*, and the phrase *over the mountains*. The object of the predicate verb *took* is *journey*, the adjuncts of which are *a* and the complex phrase *to the western part of the country*, of which *part* is the principal part; and its adjuncts are *the*, *western*, and the phrase *of the country*.

LESSON LXXX.

SYNOPSIS FOR TOPICAL REVIEW.

Etymology.—Parts of Speech.

I. Articles.
  Classes.
    1. Definite.
    2. Indefinite.

II. Nouns.
  1. Classes.
    1. Proper.
    2. Common.
      Collective.
  2. Modifications.
    1. Persons.
      1. First.
      2. Second.
      3. Third.
    2. Numbers.
      1. Singular.
      2. Plural.
    3. Genders.
      1. Masculine.
      2. Feminine.
      3. Neuter.
      4. Common.
    4. Cases.
      1. Nominative.
      2. Possessive.
      3. Objective.

III. Adjectives.
  1. Classes.
    1. Common.
    2. Proper.
    3. Numeral.
    4. Pronominal.
    5. Participial.
    6. Compound.
  2. Comparison.
    1. Positive.
    2. Comparative.
    3. Superlative.

IV. Pronouns.
  1. Classes.
    1. Personal.
      1. Simple.
      2. Compound.
    2. Relative.
      1. Simple.
      2. Compound.
    3. Interrogative.
  2. Declension.

V. Verbs.
  1. Classes.
    1. As to Signification.
      1. Active-Trans.
      2. Active-Intrans.
      3. Passive.
      4. Neuter.
    2. As to Form.
      1. Regular.
      2. Irregular.

3. Redundant.
   4. Defective.
  3. As to Use.
     Auxiliary.
 2. Modifications.
   1. Moods.
     1. Infinitive.
     2. Indicative.
     3. Potential.
     4. Subjunctive.
     5. Imperative.
   2. Tenses.
     1. Present.
     2. Imperfect.
     3. Perfect.
     4. Pluperfect.
     5. First Future.
     6. Second Future.
  3. Persons.
  4. Numbers.

VI. **Participles.**
Classes.
  1. Imperfect.
  2. Perfect.
  3. Preperfect.
VII. **Adverbs.**
  1. Classes.
    1. Of time.
    2. Of place.
    3. Of degree.
    4. Of manner.
    5. Conjunctive.
  2. Comparison.
VIII. **Conjunctions.**
Classes.
  1. Copulative.
  2. Disjunctive.
  3. Corresponsive.
IX. **Prepositions.**
X. **Interjections.**

LESSON LXXXI.

RELATION OF WORDS.

In order to be able to construct sentences properly, we must know how the words are related to each other in expressing some particular thought.

Thus, if the words *John* and *book* are to be placed together so as to express the relation of property, or ownership—that is, to denote that the book belongs to John—we say, *John's book.*

If we are to form a sentence out of the words *the, teacher, they,* and *love,* we must know the relations to be expressed. *The* evidently relates to *teacher.* Now, if *the teacher* is to be the subject and *they* the object of the verb *love,* the sentence must be, *The teacher loves them;* but if *they* is to be the subject and *the teacher* the object, the sentence must be, *They love the teacher;* thus requiring a different arrangement of the words as well as a different inflection for the verb and the pronoun.

The relations to be recognized in constructing sentences are shown in the following rules:—

RULE I.—Articles relate to the nouns which they limit.

RULE II.—Adjectives relate to nouns or pronouns.

RULE III.—Adverbs relate to verbs, participles, adjectives, or other adverbs.

RULE IV.—Participles relate to nouns or pronouns.

RULE V.—Prepositions show the relation of things.

ERRORS IN REGARD TO RELATION.

Examples.

1. *The air feels coldly.*

In this sentence the word *coldly* relates to the noun *air* as an attribute; hence it is an adjective, while it has the form of an adverb. Therefore, it should be *cold*. (Rule II.)

2. *He did it very quick.*

Here *quick*, expressing manner, relates to the verb *did;* and therefore is an adverb, while it has the form of an adjective. Hence, it should be *quickly*. (Rule III.)

3. *Give me them books.*

Here the pronoun *them* relates to *books;* but adjectives relate to nouns; therefore, *them* should be *those*. (Rule II.)

4. *I admit of what you say.*

Here the preposition *of* is used to express the relation between an active-transitive verb and its object, and this is not required; therefore, *of* should be omitted. (Rule V.)

5. *The worshiping idols is sinful.*

Here the article *the* relates to *worshiping*, which is thus used as a noun; therefore, the prepositon *of* should be inserted to express the relation between *worshiping* and *idols*. (Rules I. and V.) (See *Lesson* XXXIX.)

Exercises.

1. *Copy the following sentences, after correcting them.*
   1. Do not walk so slow.
   2. This piece of work looks very finely.
   3. The eagle flies very swift.
   4. Will you have the goodness to accept of this?
   5. How beautiful this boy writes!
   6. She wastes her time in reading of novels.
   7. He spends his time in the reading good books.
   8. He asked of the pupil several questions.
2. *Explain why each correction is made.*
3. *Analyze and parse each sentence in its correct form.*

LESSON LXXXII.

AGREEMENT OF WORDS.

In the construction of sentences, **agreement** is required in two ways.

1. Every word that has more than one form must always have that particular form which is proper to the relation in which it stands to other words; that is, its *form* must agree with its relation.

Thus, if a noun is in the possessive case, it must have the final *s* and the apostrophe before or after it; and if a personal pronoun is in the nominative case, it must have the special form of that case; and so of others.

2. Some parts of speech must agree with each other in respect to certain modifications.

Both these kinds of agreement are shown in the following rules (numbered consecutively with those of the preceding lesson) :—

RULE VI.—A noun or a pronoun which is the subject of a finite verb must be in the nominative case.

This means that it must have the *special form* of the nominative case. In English there is no practical application of this rule except in the case of pronouns, which alone have nominative and objective case forms.

The rule is confined to the *finite* verb, because when the infinitive verb has a subject it must, from the influence of the verb in the preceding clause upon which it depends, have the objective form. (See *Lesson* LXXVIII.)

RULE VII.—A noun or a personal pronoun used to explain a preceding noun or pronoun is put in the same case.

That is to say, *explanatory adjuncts agree in case* with the nouns or pronouns to which they are added; as, " My cousin, *she* that you saw, has gone home."—" I took my cousin, *her* that you met, to the station."

This case of agreement is usually called *apposition*.

RULE VIII.—A finite verb must agree with its subject in person and number.

For example, if the subject is of the third person and singular number, the verb must have the form proper to that person and number. Thus, we say, *I am, he was, we were;* not, *I be, he were, we was.*

RULE IX.—When the subject is a collective noun conveying the idea of plurality, the verb must agree with it in the plural number; but when it conveys the idea of unity, the verb must be singular.

Whether the idea conveyed is that of plurality or unity depends upon the meaning of the verb; that is, the nature of the assertion. If it refers to the individuals separately, plurality is conveyed, because there are more than one; if to the whole collectively, unity is expressed, when there is but one body referred to. Thus, in the first of the following examples, the *people consider* as individuals, not as a whole, to consider being a personal act; but, in the fifth example, the *army* as a whole was defeated, not the individuals composing it.

Examples of Plurality.

1. My people do not consider.
2. A large part of the army were drowned.
3. The public are respectfully informed.
4. The audience were greatly pleased.

Examples of Unity.

5. Pompey's army was defeated by Cæsar.
6. A fleet of many vessels was seen.
7. Has the board of commissioners adjourned?
8. A pair, of course, consists of two.

Exercises.

1. *Point out the errors in the following sentences, and copy them in the corrected form.*

1. She and me went to school together.
2. Them who do right will be rewarded.
3. You and us should feel satisfied.
4. I saw your friend, he that was with you.
5. I went with William and John, they who you know.
6. The correctness of these rules are very doubtful.
7. There was many reasons for taking that course.
8. The whole company was running away.
9. The people was duly notified of the fact.
10. The committee was deliberating upon the matter.

2. *Analyze by diagram each of the above sentences.*

3. *Prepare a written parsing exercise of the verbs, pronouns, and collective nouns.*

LESSON LXXXIII.

AGREEMENT.—VERBS AND SUBJECTS.

Rule X.—When a verb has two or more subjects connected by *and*, it must agree with them in the plural number; as, "Temperance and exercise *preserve* health."— "William, James, and John *have been promoted.*"

The following are exceptions:—

1. When the nouns connected refer to the same person or thing, the verb should be singular; as, "This patriot, statesman, and orator *was* famous."

2. When the connected subjects are each preceded by the adjective *each, every,* or *no,* they are taken separately, and require a singular verb; as, "And every sense and every heart *is* joy."

Rule XI.—When a verb has two or more singular subjects connected by *or* or *nor*, it must agree with them in the singular number; as, "Fear or jealousy *affects* him."

If the connected subjects differ in person or number, the verb should be made to agree with that which is placed next to it; as, "Neither he nor his brothers *were* present."—"Neither you nor I *am* concerned."

Sometimes, however, it is better to express the verb or the proper auxiliary in connection with each subject; as, "Either thou *art* to blame, or I *am.*"

When the subjects include the speaker or writer, he should be mentioned last, unless the predicate is the confession of a fault; as, "My friend and I are invited.—" I and my brother Robert are to blame."

Exercises.

Correct, analyze, and parse the following sentences.
1. Industry and frugality leads to wealth.
2. Either ability or inclination were wanting.
3. Neither John nor his brother have been to school.
4. My love and esteem toward him remains unaltered.
5. Either he or I are mistaken. (*Express in two ways.*)
6. No pains nor cost were spared in his education.
7. Neither John nor I were to blame.
8. Every boy and every girl were at play.
9. No wife, no mother, and no child were there to comfort him.
10. That brilliant patriot, soldier, and statesman have passed from earth.

PUNCTUATION.—See *Lesson* XXV.

LESSON LXXXIV.

AGREEMENT.—CONNECTED VERBS.

RULE XII.—When verbs are connected by a conjunction, they must either agree in mood, tense, and form, or have separate subjects; as, "She *played* and *sung* admirably." "He *was* good, and he *will receive* his reward."

The following tenses are often connected without repeating the subject:—

1. The present, perfect, and first-future tenses of the indicative mood.
2. The corresponding tenses of the indicative and potential moods.

The affirmative and negative forms, and the simple and compound forms are, also, often excepted. In the latter case, the simple verb should generally be placed first. Thus:—

AGREEMENT.—SUBJECT AND ATTRIBUTE. 131

"What nothing earthly *gives* or *can destroy.*"—*Pope.*
"Some *are* and *must be*, greater than the rest."—*Id.*
Auxiliaries and other words common to several verbs are usually expressed to the first only, being understood to the rest. Thus:—
"Every sincere endeavor to amend *shall be* assisted, [*shall be*] accepted, and [*shall be*] rewarded."
"You have *seen it*, but I have not" [*seen it*].

Exercises.

Correct, analyze, and parse the following sentences.
1. He was invited to the meeting but would not attend.
2. William can learn his lesson, but will not.
3. They would neither go in themselves, nor suffered others to enter.
4. He had arranged to leave the country, but could not go.
5. Did he not waste his time and neglected his lessons?

LESSON LXXXV.

AGREEMENT.—SUBJECT AND ATTRIBUTE.

RULE XIII.—The attribute must agree in case with the subject; as, "It was *she.*"—"*Who* is he?"—"*Whom* did he allege it to be?"—"Art thou *he?*"

In interrogative sentences, the attribute is usually placed before the verb, and the subject after it; as, "*Who* art thou?" Or the subject and attribute are both placed after the verb; as, "Art thou *he?*"—"Am I thy *slave?*"

The verb *be* generally affirms only the connection between the subject and attribute. When the latter is a noun, it may express:
1. *Class;* as, "Cain was a *murderer.*"—2. *Identity;* as, "Cain was the *murderer* of Abel."

Class or identity is sometimes affirmed by other verbs, in connection with a particular act or state of being; as, "She *looked* a goddess, and she *walked* a queen."—" It *seemed* a miracle."—" He *became* a scholar." Also by affirming not only the connection but the cause or manner of its establishment; as, " The twig *has grown* a tree."—" He *was elected* president."—" The child was named John."

When the active verb is used instead of the passive, the object is an infinitive clause. (See *Lesson* LXXVIII.) For example, "They elected *him president*."—"They named *the child John*."—" The saints proclaim *thee King*." In these cases the predicate verb which usually connects the subject and the attribute is the infinitive of *be*, understood.

The attribute is sometimes used in an infinitive phrase without reference to any particular subject; as, " To be a *poet* requires genius."—" To be *good* is to be *happy*."

Exercises.

Correct, analyze, and parse the following sentences.

1. It could not have been her that I saw.
2. They believed it to be I, but it was my brother.
3. Let him be whom he may, I will have him punished.
4. Who do they think him to be?
5. Whom do they say that I am?
6. It was me who wrote the letter which you thought to be from your friend.
7. I should have acted in the same way, if I had been him.

LESSON LXXXVI.

AGREEMENT.—PRONOUN AND ANTECEDENT.

RULE XIV.—A pronoun must agree with its antecedent, or the noun or pronoun which it represents, in person, number, and gender; as, *I, who am* your friend, will aid you."

AGREEMENT.—PRONOUN AND ANTECEDENT.

While every pronoun must represent some noun or pronoun, expressed or understood, it is only the relative pronoun that necessarily has an *antecedent* (word *going before*).

The pronoun must always agree with the noun or pronoun which it represents, whether it be an antecedent or not.

The antecedent of a relative pronoun is always in the same sentence; but it is in the principal clause, while the relative is in the dependent clause.

Who is applied only to persons, and *which* to brute animals or inanimate things.

That may be used to represent either.

The relative pronoun should be placed as near as possible to the antecedent.

The pronoun *it* is often used indefinitely; as, "It rains."—"It is stormy."

It is also very often used to represent a phrase or a clause coming after the verb; as, "It is good *to be here*."

The phrase in this case is an explanatory adjunct of the pronoun. (See *Lesson* LXXIX.)

As is sometimes used as a relative pronoun; as, "Avoid such *as* are vicious."

RULE XV.—When the antecedent is a collective noun conveying the idea of plurality, the pronoun must agree with it in the plural number; but when it conveys the idea of unity, the pronoun should be singular.

Examples of Plurality.

The council disagreed in *their* sentiments.
The people will not relinquish *their* rights.
The general orders the army to lay down *their* arms.

Examples of Unity.

The nation will enforce all its laws.
The association expelled two of its members.
The committee has made its report.
The army continued its retreat.

Exercises.

Correct, parse, and analyze the following sentences.
1. The party disagreed in its views of the measure.
2. Every one must judge of their own feelings.
3. Each of us should strive to do all we can.
4. The lion who seemed so fierce was brought from Africa.
5. The court by their decision have closed the case.
6. The senate will consider the matter at their next session.
7. The meeting showed its approbation by applause.
8. The new board of directors have elected their officers.

LESSON LXXXVII.

AGREEMENT.—CONNECTED ANTECEDENTS.

RULE XVI.—When a pronoun has two or more antecedents connected by *and*, it must agree with them in the plural number; as, "*James* and *John* will favor us with their company."

When the antecedents are of different persons, use the first person rather than the second, and the second rather than the third; as, "You, William, and I must make our excuses."

The exceptions and observations under Rule X. are applicable to antecedents as well as subjects.

RULE XVII.—When a pronoun has two or more singular antecedents connected by *or* or *nor*, it must agree with them in the singular number; as, "James or John will favor us with *his* company."

When a pronoun is used to represent antecedents of different genders, the masculine should be used rather than the feminine; as, "Neither Sarah nor James will give up *his* place." The use of the expression "his or her" is awkward. The difficulty may be avoided by a change in the construction; as, "Sarah will not give up her place, nor James his."

Exercises.

Correct, analyze, and parse the following sentences.
1. Truth and honesty will never fail of its reward.
2. One or the other must relinquish their claim.
3. Neither John nor Peter appear to have learned their lessons.
4. You and your sister should obey their parents.
5. Neither the watch nor the chain was ever found by their owner.
6. Cherish love and unity, for it is the source of all happiness.
7. Every plant, every flower, and every animal show the wisdom of their Creator.
8. Neither Mary nor her brother complied with their teacher's request.

LESSON LXXXVIII.

GOVERNMENT.

When a word standing in a certain relation to another word is required on that account to undergo some inflection or modification, the word thus inflected or modified is said to be *governed* by the other word.

Thus, if the word *John* stands in the relation of ownership to the word *book*, it is governed by the latter in the possessive case, and must assume the possessive inflection ('s), thus, *John's book.*

Thus, too, a preposition coming before a noun or a pronoun governs it in the objective case; as, To *him*, for *her*, from *them*.

RULE XVIII.—A noun or a pronoun in the possessive case is governed by the name of the thing possessed; as, "*Your* pencil is not as sharp as *mine*."—"The credit is *mine*, not *theirs*."

Every noun in the possessive case requires the sign of possession except when two or more nouns are connected by a conjunction, and the person or thing possessed by each is the same. Then the sign of possession is required by that only which immediately precedes the governing word. Thus :—

1. Cain and Abel's parents were Adam and Eve.
2. Was John and William's father aware of his sons' conduct?
3. Henry's and Samuel's parents were unknown to each other.
4. Cain's occupation and Abel's [occupation] were unlike.
5. Neither James's nor Charles's teacher was very successful.

Rule XIX.—Active-transitive verbs and their imperfect and preperfect participles govern the objective case; as, "I found *her* assisting *him*."

An active-transitive verb is often followed by the direct object of the action and the *indirect object*, or that in regard to which the action is performed; as, "He gave *her* the book."—"I paid *him* the money."

The indirect object is usually governed by a preposition understood; as, "I paid [to] him the money."

When, in such cases, a passive verb is formed from the active-transitive verb, the direct object should be made the subject; as, "The book was given to her."—"The money was paid to him."

An active-transitive verb sometimes has two objects, both of which may be deemed direct, one being the name of a person and the other that of a thing; as, "I taught the *boy grammar*."—"He asked *them* a *question*."

When this construction is changed to the passive form, either object may be made the subject, the other still retaining its relation to the action expressed by the verb, and, of course, remaining in the same case; "The boy was taught *grammar*."

An active-transitive verb is sometimes followed by an object and an attribute agreeing with it, the predicate verb being understood; as, "Thy saints proclaim *thee King*." This is the reverse of the passive construction, "Thou art proclaimed King by thy saints."

Exercises.

Correct, analyze, and parse the following sentences.

1. John's and William's father chided them for their misconduct.
2. Adam was Cain's and Abel's father.
3. I have seen neither William nor Charles's book.
4. Brown and Jones's houses will soon be occupied.
5. She I shall more readily forgive.
6. My father allowed my brother and I to go with him.
7. Who should I meet last week but my old friend.
8. They who disobey the rules the teacher will punish.

LESSON LXXXIX.

GOVERNMENT.—PREPOSITIONS.

Rule XX.—Prepositions govern the objective case; as, "No one was seen by *him* except *her* and *me*."

After the adjectives *like*, *near*, and *nigh*, the preposition *to* or *unto* is generally understood; as, "Near [*to*] him was his friend." "His brother was like [*unto*] him."

Nouns of *time* or *measure*, when connected with verbs or adjectives, are generally used without a governing preposition; as "We walked [?] several *miles*." "The wall is ten *feet* high;" that is, *high* [*to*, or *to the extent of*] *ten feet*.

The infinitive mood is frequently the object of the preposition *to*. (See *Lesson* LXXVII.)

After the active verbs *bid, dare, feel, hear, let, make, need, see*, and their participles, the infinitive mood is generally used without the preposition *to;* as "They *bade* him *go*." "We *dare* not *do* it." "I *felt* it touch *me*."

The auxiliary *be* of the passive infinitive is also suppressed after *feel, hear, make*, and *see;* as "I heard the letter *read*."

Exercises.

Correct, analyze, and parse the following sentences.
1. Let that remain a secret between you and I.
2. Who did you give the message to?
3. Did you not see him to strike his brother?
4. Bid all the boys to come in without any further delay.
5. Can I not make this matter to be clearly understood by you?

LESSON XC.
DEFINITIONS.—REVIEW.

That part of grammar which treats of the construction of sentences is called **syntax**.

From the Greek *syn*, together; and *taxis*, arrangement.

Syntax treats of the relation, agreement, government, and arrangement of words in sentences.

The **relation** of words is their dependence, or connection, according to the sense.

The **agreement** of words is their similarity in person, number, gender, case, mood, tense, or form.

The **government** of words is that power which one word has over another to cause it to assume some particular modification.

The **arrangement** of words is their relative place in the sentence.

The **rules of syntax** are designed to guide in the application of the principles of grammar to the construction of sentences.

False syntax is a violation, in the construction of sentences, of any of the rules or methods of speech proper to the language.

Every language has its peculiar rules of syntax and methods of speech, including modifications and forms, or inflections. The principles and methods of analysis are common to all languages.

Review Questions.

What are the rules that refer to relation? What are those that relate to agreement? What are those that relate to government? In how many ways is agreement required? What is apposition? How does a verb agree with a collective noun? When is the idea conveyed singular? When plural? Give examples of each. How does a verb agree with two or more subjects? How should connected verbs agree? What exceptions are there to the general rule? With what must the attribute agree? How should a pronoun agree with its antecedent? How with two or more connected antecedents? How are nouns or pronouns in the possessive case governed? When may the sign of possession be omitted? What do active-transitive verbs govern? What is the difference between the direct and the indirect object? What do prepositions govern? How are nouns of time and measure governed? How is the infinitive mood governed? When is the infinitive mood used without *to?* Does the word *to* always govern the infinitive? Give examples.

LESSON XCI.

DIFFERENT KINDS OF CLAUSES.

Clauses, like sentences, may be **simple, complex,** or **compound.**

Complex and compound sentences are sometimes called *members.* Every complex or compound clause would be a complex or compound sentence if it were used by itself.

A principal clause and one or more dependent clauses form a **complex sentence.** (See *Lesson* LIV.)

A **dependent clause** is the subject, object, or attribute in the sentence, or else is an adjunct to some word in the principal clause.

Dependent clauses, when used as adjuncts, are connected to the principal clause by relative pronouns or conjunctive adverbs.

When clauses are connected by conjunctions they form **compound sentences.**

The clauses of a compound sentence may be independent as regards the *grammatical structure* of the sentence, or one may be subordinate to the other in regard to the thought or fact expressed. In the two following sentences the clauses are wholly independent, and their order of arrangement might be reversed:—

"He rode all unarmed, and he rode all alone." "Riches have wings, and grandeur is a dream."

In the following sentences the arrangement is dictated only by the order of time, and the clauses are independent:—

"He quaffed off the wine, and he threw down the cup." "All flesh is grass, and all its glory fades."

The clauses of a compound sentence that are connected without any dependence are called **co-ordinate clauses.**

When a compound sentence is not composed of co-ordinate clauses, it must consist of a **leading clause** and one or more **subordinate clauses.**

The following are examples:—
1. "I will visit him, if he be sick."
2. "You must take heed, lest you be betrayed."
3. "I shall not go, unless I receive a notice, and unless the weather be favorable."

In Sentences 1 and 2 the second clause is subordinate, and in 3 the second and third clauses are subordinate. In these sentences there are no *adjunct clauses*, and no clause forms a part of the structure of any other clause. The sentences, therefore, are not complex but compound.

For exercises on clauses see the following lessons.

LESSON XCII.

SUBJECT AND ATTRIBUTE CLAUSES.

(Complex Sentences.)

Analyze the following sentences by diagram and orally. Write the parsing of 1, 2, *and* 3.

1. That you have wronged me is very evident.
2. That we should be kind to all is without dispute.
3. That idleness leads to ruin is a certain fact.
4. How this difficulty is to be removed has not been discovered.
5. My hope is that you will be restored to health.
6. His reply was that he was sure of success.
7. The general sentiment was that the accused person was guilty.

EXAMPLE.—"That Cæsar invaded Britain is a well-known historical fact."

Cæsar ---- invaded ---- Britain
―――――――――――――――――――――― (that) ----- is | fact.
                                          a
                                          well-known
                                          historical

ORAL ANALYSIS.—A complex declarative sentence. The subject is the dependent clause, *Cæsar invaded Britain ;* the predicate verb is *is* ; the attribute is *fact.* The connective word is *that.* The subject of the dependent clause is *Cæsar*, the predicate verb *invaded*, and the object *Britain.*

OBSERVATION.

The word *that*, which introduces these clauses, is considered a conjunction, because, while it does not connect two complete propositions, it implies that the clause which it introduces is dependent upon, and forms a part of, the principal proposition.

OBJECT CLAUSES.

MODEL EXERCISE IN WRITTEN PARSING.*

Word.	Part of Speech.	Class.	Modifications.	Relation.	Syntax.
That	Conj.	Copulative.		Connects clauses.	
Cæsar	Noun.	Proper.	3d, Sing., Mas., Nom.	Subj. of Invaded.	Rule VI.
Invaded	Verb.	Regular. Act.-Trans.	Ind., Imp., 3d, Sing.	Pred. Verb.	Rule VIII.
Britain	Noun.	Proper.	3d, Sing., Neut., Obj.	Obj. of Invaded.	Rule XIX.
Is	Verb.	Irregular. Neuter.	Ind., Pres., 3d, Sing.	Pred. Verb.	Rule VI.
A	Article.	Indef.		Adjunct of *fact*.	Rule I.
Well-known	Adj.	Compound.		" " "	Rule II.
Historical	"	Common.		" " "	Rule II.
Fact.	Noun.	Common.	3d, Sing., Neut., Nom.	Attribute.	Rule XIII.

CONSTRUCTION.

Construct three sentences, each containing a subject clause.
Construct three sentences, each containing an attribute clause.

LESSON XCIII.

OBJECT CLAUSES.

Analyze the following complex sentences by diagram and orally.

1. The orator felt that every eye was upon him.
2. Remember that indolence can lead to nothing but disgrace and misery.
3. The fool hath said in his heart, There is no God.
4. Consider well whether you are able to accomplish the work undertaken.
5. Nathan said unto David, Thou art the man.
6. Catharine had now to learn what it is to be a slave.

---

* This form of parsing exercise is a tabulated representation of Goold Brown's oral method. See *Grammar of English Grammars*, page 475, and on other pages.

INFINITIVE OBJECT CLAUSES.

EXAMPLE.—"Always bear in mind that you owe very much to your parents."

[diagram of sentence]

OBSERVATIONS.

[The numbers refer to the sentences.]

2. In this sentence *but* is used as a preposition.

6. Here the object clause depends upon the principal part (*learn*) of the infinitive phrase, which itself is the object of the verb *had* (that is, *had as a task*). In this phrase, *to be a slave* is an explanatory adjunct of the subject *it*. *What* is the attribute. The diagram of it is here given:—

[diagram]

In this phrase, *slave* is an indefinite attribute. (See *Lesson* LXXXV., Obs. under Rule XIII.)

CONSTRUCTION.

Construct five sentences, each containing an object clause.

LESSON XCIV.

INFINITIVE OBJECT CLAUSES.

Analyze, by diagram and orally, the following complex sentences. (See *Lesson* LXXVIII.) *Parse Sentences 5 and 6.*

1. Many witnesses proved him to be guilty of the crime of which he was accused.
2. Do not forbid them to enter the garden.

144   INFINITIVE OBJECT CLAUSES.

3. A good speaker will always make himself understood by his audience.
4. William made himself very agreeable in society.
5. Let the child learn such things as are adapted to his understanding.
6. We often see bad men honored by official appointment.

EXAMPLE.—Sentence 1.

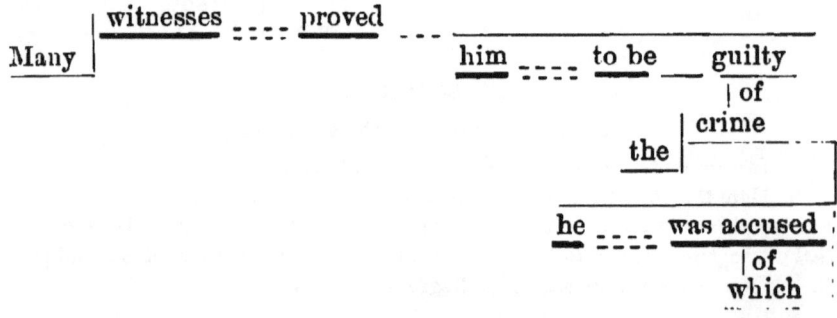

ORAL ANALYSIS.—A complete declarative sentence. The subject noun is *witnesses*, modified by the adjunct *many*; the predicate verb is *proved*, and its object the infinitive clause, of which *him* is the subject, *to be* the verb, and *guilty* the attribute, modified by the complex prepositional phrase, *of the crime of which he was accused.* Of this phrase the principal part is *crime*, of which the adjuncts are *the* and the relative clause, *of which he was accused.*

OBSERVATIONS.

3. The infinitive verb in this sentence is *to be understood.* The subject of the infinitive after *make* and some other verbs is sometimes called a *factitive object;* as, "He made the *horse* run rapidly."—"It made the *water* red." —"He made the *water* wine."—"He painted the *blinds* green." (The word *factitive* is from the Latin *facere*, to make.)

The relation in which the noun or adjective, in this construction, stands to the preceding noun or pronoun is that of an attribute to the subject, the connecting verb being omitted. A change to the passive form will render this obvious; as, "The *horse* was made *to run.*"—"The *water* was made *red.*"— "'The *water* was made *wine.*"—"The *blinds* were painted *green.*"

4. "Made himself very agreeable;" that is, *made* or *caused himself to be very agreeable.*

5. In this sentence *as* is used as a relative pronoun. (See *Lesson* LXXXVI., Obs. under Rule XIV.)

CONSTRUCTION.

Construct five sentences, each containing an infinitive object clause.

LESSON XCV.

ADJECTIVE CLAUSES.

Analyze, by diagram and orally, the following complex sentences. Parse Sentences 6 and 8.

1. No person who is truly honest will in any way deceive.
2. Xerxes, who invaded Greece, was a great monarch.
3. The statement that the vessel was lost proved untrue.
4. The merchant received intelligence that his agent had defrauded him.
5. The promise that he should be appointed to an office was not fulfilled.
6. Why should he ever be afraid who fully trusts in the lovingkindness of the Almighty?
7. He never lost confidence that the truth would finally triumph.
8. I visited last year the place where I was born.

EXAMPLE.—"I, who am your friend, will aid you in the task which you have undertaken."

```
I  _____  will aid  _____  you
                     | in
                     | task
              the    |_____
                     | You ____ have undertaken ____ | which
  who ____ am        | friend
            your     |
```

OBSERVATIONS.

1 and 2. For explanation of the punctuation of the relative clauses, see *Lessons* XLIX. and LIV.

3. The word *that* is a conjunction, and the clause which it introduces shows what statement is spoken of.

8. The phrase *last year* is adverbial and prepositional, the preposition being understood. *Where I was born* is an adjective clause because it is an adjunct of *place*. *Where* is an adverb relating to the verb *was born*, and is equivalent to the adverbial phrase *in which*. The adverb *where* is also connective.

LESSON XCVI.

ADVERBIAL CLAUSES.

Analyze, by diagram and orally, the following complex sentences. Parse Sentences 3 and 4.

1. He would not rest until his work was finished.
2. Loose conversation operates on the mind as poison does on the body.
3. While the battle went on the enemy's artillery continued to fire on the advancing troops.
4. My friend, immediately after he returned home, paid me a visit, which was very agreeable.
5. Where your treasure is, there will your heart be also.
6. When they came to countries where the people were simple and unwarlike, they took possession.

EXAMPLE.—" When faith grows dim, and hope has fled, how sad it is to live !"

NOTE.—Do not forget that the *parallel lines* indicate the explanatory or appositive relation.

ORAL ANALYSIS.—A complex exclamatory sentence. The subject is *it;* the predicate verb, *is;* and the attribute, *sad.* The subject has the explanatory adjunct *to live;* the predicate verb is modified by the compound adverbial clause, *when faith grows dim* and *hope has fled,* consisting of the two simple clauses connected by *and.*

When is a conjunctive adverb connecting the principal clause and the dependent clauses, and relating to the verbs *grows* and *has fled.*

The diagram shows this connection by the line continuing the adjunct line from *is;* and the twofold relation is shown by the adjunct line from *grows* and *has fled.*

EXPLANATORY CLAUSES.

OBSERVATIONS.

4. Before *home* the preposition *to* is understood. (See *Lesson* LXXXVIII., Obs. under Rule XIX.) *Me* is also an indirect object.

5. The adverb *there*, corresponding to *where*, is used only for emphasis. It introduces the principal clause, which ordinarily is placed first.

6. *Where* is equivalent to *in which*. (See *Lesson* XCV., Obs. 8.)

PUNCTUATION.—Adverbial phrases and clauses when out of their ordinary or natural position should be separated by the comma. (See Sentences 4, 5, 6.)

LESSON XCVII.

EXPLANATORY CLAUSES.

Analyze, by diagram and orally, the following complex sentences. Parse Sentences 4 and 5.

1. It has been conclusively proved that the earth is round.
2. It is the wish of most parents that their children should be well educated.
3. It caused much anxiety that he should have absented himself so long.
4. Would it not be advisable that you should give up the project?
5. It was observed that he derived but little enjoyment from the benefits which he diffused.

EXAMPLE.—" Explain, when you are able, how it happened that you did not foresee what occurred."

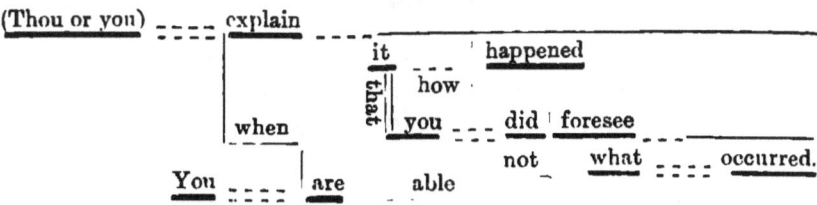

ORAL ANALYSIS.—A complex imperative sentence. The subject is *thou* or *you* (understood); the predicate verb, *explain;* and the object *how it happened.* The adjunct of *explain* is the adverbial clause, *when you are able;*

and the adjunct of *it* is the complex clause, *you did not foresee what occurred*, connected to the principal clause by *that*. The clause *what occurred* is the object of *foresee*.

OBSERVATIONS.

5. In this sentence *but* is an adverbial adjunct of *little*, being equivalent to *only*. The explanatory clause is complex, containing the modifying relative clause, *which he diffused*.

CONSTRUCTION.

Construct five sentences, each containing an explanatory clause.

LESSON XCVIII.

INDEPENDENT CLAUSES AND PHRASES.

A clause may be treated as independent when it is intended to form no part of the general structure of the sentence. The following are examples.

1. Such, *said I*, is the vanity of all earthly ambition.
2. Endeavor, *I beseech you*, to store your minds with that knowledge which will ever be useful to you.
3. "Almet," *said he*, "remember what thou hast seen."
4. However dangerous idleness may be, are there not pleasures, *it may be asked*, that attend it?

Such clauses are sometimes called *parenthetical clauses*. Independent phrases have various forms:

1. *Infinitive;* as, "*To confess the truth*, I was wrong."
2. *Participial;* as, "*Generally speaking*, that is true."
3. *Vocative* (addressing); as, "*My dear son*, avoid bad company."
4. *Absolute;* as, "*Night coming on*, we sought a place of shelter."
5. *Pleonastic;* as, "*Your fathers*, where are they?"

In the last construction there is an excess of words *(pleonasm)*, used for the purpose of emphasis. The last example simply expressed would be : *Where are your fathers ?* But by making the phrase *your fathers* independent, we render it emphatic.

All independent nouns and pronouns are in the *nominative case.*

PUNCTUATION.—Independent words, phrases, and clauses are to be set off by commas. (See examples.)

EXAMPLES ANALYZED.

1. "Such, said I, is the vanity of all earthly ambition."

```
    I  ---- said
              vanity ---- is ---- such
       the    of
              ambition
        all
      earthly
```

As this diagram shows, the independent clause may be treated as the principal clause, and the main proposition be considered as an object clause. This, however, while grammatically correct, does not properly interpret the true relation of the parts, as it makes that the primary proposition which is designed to be only subordinate.

2. "The sun having set, we were obliged to discontinue our observations."

```
         sun
    The     having set
         we  ------  were obliged
                       to
                     discontinue  ----  observations.
                              our
```

Analyze in the same manner all the examples in this lesson, and parse the independent clauses and phrases.

CONSTRUCTION.

Construct three sentences, each containing an independent clause, and three sentences each containing an independent phrase.

LESSON XCIX.

COMPOUND SENTENCES.

Analyze the following compound sentences by diagram and orally. State of what kinds of clauses they are composed. (*See Lesson* XCI.)

1. The clouds of sorrow gathered round his head, and the tempest of hatred roared about his dwelling.
2. Science may raise thee to eminence, but religion alone can guide thee to felicity.
3. If thou go, see that thou offend not.
4. Discover not a secret to another, lest he that heareth it put thee to shame.
5. Happiness is more equally diffused among mankind than most persons suppose.
6. While every one praises truth and sincerity, how few there are who constantly practice them!
7. The secrets of nature remain so long undiscovered because so many think they know them.
8. When good men rule, the people rejoice; but they mourn under the tyranny of the vicious.
9. Industry brings pleasure; idleness, pain.
10. Favor is deceitful, and beauty is vain; but a woman that feareth the Lord, she shall be praised.

EXAMPLE.—"No man of sense ever took any pains to appear wise, as no honest man ever used tricks to display his own integrity."

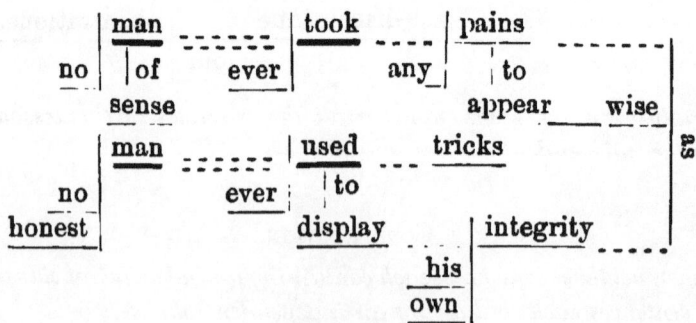

OBSERVATIONS.

3. Leading and subordinate clauses; subordinate clause introduced by *if*. Leading clause complex.
4. The first clause is the leading clause. The subordinate clause is complex. *Put* is the subjunctive mood.
5. The second clause is subordinate by comparison, expressed by *than*.
7. The second clause expresses the cause of what is asserted in the first as a *leading proposition*. The relation expressed is that of cause and effect.
9. The predicate verb of the second clause is understood. The comma is used to mark its omission.
10. The first part of the second clause of the sentence, *a woman that feareth the Lord*, is independent by pleonasm.

PUNCTUATION.—1. The semicolon is used to separate clauses when they are divided by commas. (See Sentences 8, 9, and 10.)
2. The comma is used to supply an omitted predicate verb, as in Sentence 9.

LESSON C.

SYNOPSIS FOR TOPICAL REVIEW.

Analysis.

[The numbers refer to those of the lessons.]

I. Sentences 18, 19
  I. Classes 48
    1. As to Form 48
      1. Simple 48
      2. Complex 54
      3. Compound 48
    2. As to Use 32
      1. Declarative 32
      2. Interrogative ... 32
      3. Imperative 33
      4. Exclamatory ... 34
  II. Parts 30
    1. Subject 30
      Noun or pronoun .. 30
      Simple or compound 37
    2. Predicate 30
      1. Verb 30
      2. Object 21
      3. Attribute 36
      Simple or compound 37
    3. Adjuncts 30
      1. Classes 52
        1. As to Form ... 52
          1. Word 52
          2. Phrase 52
          3. Clause 52

152 SYNOPSIS FOR TOPICAL REVIEW

    2. As to Use....52
       1. Adjective ..52
       2. Adverbial ..30
                  52, 53
       3. Explanatory 52
    3. As to Signification......52
       1. Modifying..52
       2. Descriptive.52

II. Phrases...............38
    Classes...........38, 79
    1. As to Form.......38
       1. Prepositional...38
       2. Participial......76
       3. Infinitive.......77
    2. As to Use........79
       1. Substantive
          (Noun).......79
          1. Subject......79
          2. Object.......79
          3. Attribute.....79
       2. Adjective.......79
       3. Adverbial......79
       4. Explanatory....79
       5. Independent...79
    3. As to Construction.79
       1. Simple.........79
       2. Complex..... 79
       3. Compound.....79

III. Clauses...............91
    Classes................91
    1. As to Form.......91
       1. Relative........54
       2. Infinitive object.78
    2. As to Use........91
       1. Substantive
          (Noun).......91
          1. Subject......91
          2. Object.......91
          3. Attribute....91
       2. Adjective......91
       3. Adverbial......91
       4. Explanatory....91
       5. Independent, or Parenthetical.91
       6. Independent.53, 91
    3. As to relation, or Connections....91
       { 1. Principal.....53
       { 2. Dependent....53
       { 1. Leading..... 91
       { 2. Subordinate...91
       { 3. Co-ordinate ...91
       { 1. Independent ..91
       { 2. Subordinate ..91
    4. As to construction.91
       1. Simple.......91
    Members. { 2. Complex......91
               { 3. Compound....91

LESSON CI.

USE OF CAPITALS.

Capitals should be used in the following cases:

1. In the titles of books, and in the heads of their principal divisions.

EXAMPLES.—Pope's Essay on Man.—Brown's Grammar of the English Language.—The Acts of the Apostles.—The Analysis of Sentences.

2. The first word of every sentence, or of any clause or phrase separately numbered, should begin with a capital.

EXAMPLE.—Parents should teach their children: 1. The duty of obedience; 2. The importance of industry; 3. The need of perseverance.

3. Names of the Deity should always begin with a capital.

EXAMPLES.—God, Jehovah, the Almighty, the Supreme Being, Providence, the All-Wise, the Father, the Great First Cause.

Remark.—Pronouns referring to the Deity need not begin with a capital unless they are used emphatically; as, "Shall He who created the ear not hear?" "The Deity revealed himself to Moses."

4. Proper nouns and adjectives, and all titles of office and honor should begin with a capital.

EXAMPLES.—The city of London is the capital of the British Empire.—The President of the United States.—New York is situated on the Hudson river.—The prophet Elisha.—The Copernican system.

5. The letters I and O, when used by themselves as words, should be capitals.

EXAMPLE.—"Out of the depths have I cried unto thee, O Lord."

6. Every line in a poem should begin with a capital.

EXAMPLE.—" To others do (the law is not severe)
What to thyself thou wishest to be done."

7. A direct and complete quotation should begin with a capital

EXAMPLES.—Virgil says, "Labor conquers all things."—Nathan said to David: "Thou art the man."—"I will not," said John, "degrade myself by telling a falsehood."

Exercise.

Copy the following sentences, and insert or omit capital letters as required.

1. Bancroft's history of the United states is a great work.
2. The roman empire was divided into two parts on the death of theodosius.
3. The theban General, epaminondas, was noted for his love of truth.
4. The "lady of the lake" was written by sir Walter scott, a noted scottish writer and poet.
5. Pope says, "order is heaven's First law."
6. "O liberty!" exclaimed cicero, the roman orator, "o Sound once delightful to every roman ear."
7. "Society, friendship, and love,
  divinely bestowed upon man!
 o, had i the wings of a Dove,
  how soon would i taste you again!"

LESSON CII.

PUNCTUATION.—REVIEW.

Directions have been given in the preceding lessons for the use of the points. The following is a summary of the rules, chiefly for review and guidance in the succeeding lessons.

The **comma** is required to separate—

1. The simple clauses of a compound sentence. (See *Lessons* XXV., XXXVII., and LV.)

2. Dependent clauses and phrases, when merely descriptive. (See *Lesson* LII.)

3. A series of three or more words used in the same construction. (See *Lessons* XXV., and XXXVII.)

4. Words and phrases in apposition. (See *Lesson* LII.)

5. Relative clauses when not used as modifying adjuncts. (See *Lesson* LIV.)

6. Participial phrases not used as modifying adjuncts. (See *Lesson* LXXVI.)

7. Phrases and clauses placed out of their natural order. (See *Lessons* LXXVI. and XCVI.)

8. Independent words, phrases, and clauses. (See *Lessons* XL. and XCVIII.)

9. Words between which there is a predicate verb understood. (See *Lesson* XCIX.)

The **semicolon** is required to separate compound or complex clauses. (See *Lesson* XCIX.)

The **colon** is used chiefly to separate quotations and examples, as in the following :—

1. Always heed the golden rule: "Do unto others as you would have them do unto you."

2. Cherish the three cardinal virtues : faith, hope, and charity.

The **period** should be used—

1. At the end of every sentence.

2. After an abbreviated word; as, "Jno. A. Smith."—"Gibbon's Hist., vol. ii., p. 155."

The **note of interrogation** is used to denote a question.

The **note of exclamation** is used to indicate some strong or sudden emotion. (See *Lessons* XXVII. and XXXIV.)

The **dash** is used—

1. To denote a break or unexpected pause; as, "Didst thou— but how can I ask thee?"

2. To separate parenthetical expressions; as, "Religion is— who doubts it?—the greatest of themes."

3. Before explanatory expressions; as, "There are two kinds of evils—those which can be cured, and those which cannot."

The **curves,** or **marks of parenthesis,** enclose parenthetical expressions.

EXAMPLE.—"How often do we see a gentleman (if gentleman he can be called) commit an act of rude selfishness!"

The **brackets** or **crotchets** are used to enclose some correction or explanation.

EXAMPLE.—"He [who?] was of a different opinion."

LESSON CIII.

EXERCISES IN CONSTRUCTION.

Construct sentences, one of each kind, containing—

I. PHRASES.

1. Two prepositional phrases. 2. An explanatory infinitive phrase. 3. An independent phrase (infinitive). 4. An independent phrase (absolute). 5. An independent phrase (vocative). (See *Lesson* XCVIII.) 6. A complex adverbial phrase. 7. A complex participial phrase. 8. A compound adjective phrase. 9. An infinitive phrase used as a subject. 10. An infinitive phrase used as an object. 11. An infinitive phrase used as an attribute. 12. An infinitive phrase used as an adjective adjunct.

II. CLAUSES. (*See Preceding Lessons.*)

13. A subject clause. 14. An object clause. 15. An attribute clause. 16. An adverbial clause. 17. An explanatory clause. 18. An adjective clause (modifying). 19. An adjective clause (descriptive). 20. An independent (parenthetical clause). 21. A principal clause and two dependent clauses. 22. Three independent clauses. 23. A leading and a subordinate clause. 24. Two complex clauses. 25. Two compound clauses.

LESSON CIV.

COMPOSITION.—CONNECTION OF SENTENCES.

Sentences, when they are related in thought, may be connected so as to form a composition.

The following is an example :—
1. Charles was a boy about seven years old.
2. He was in very poor health.
3. The doctor recommended a change of air.
4. Charles was sent on a visit to his aunt.
5. She lived on a farm in the country.
6. Charles was delighted to see so many new things.
7. He took much pleasure in watching the milking of the cows, and the feeding of the pigs and poultry.
8. He roamed over the fields and through the groves.
9. He often went with his cousin to the brook, and spent many hours fishing in it.
10. He had a very pleasant time.
11. After a couple of months, he returned home strong and well.

These sentences united form the following composition on—

Charles's Visit to the Country.

Charles was a boy about seven years old, and, as he was in very poor health, the doctor recommended a change of air. Charles was, therefore, sent on a visit to his aunt, who lived on a farm in the country. He was delighted to see so many new things, and took much pleasure in watching the milking of the cows, and the feeding of the pigs and poultry. He roamed over the fields and through the groves; and often went with his cousin to the brook, and spent many hours fishing in it. He had, indeed, a very pleasant time, and returned home quite strong and well.

Classify the sentences, and write the name of each. Which of them are connected in the composition? What connecting words are employed?

158 COMPOSITION.—CONNECTION OF SENTENCES.

Exercises.

In a similar way, write compositions by uniting the sentences given.

I. The Dog of Ulysses.

1. Ulysses was King of ancient Ithaca.
2. Ithaca is an island near Greece.
3. Ulysses joined the Greeks in their famous war against Troy.
4. Troy was taken after a siege of ten years.
5. Ulysses could not return home till after many years of wandering and adventure.
6. When at last he got back, he found his kingdom in the possession of enemies.
7. He put on the disguise of a beggar.
8. No one knew him thus disguised, and after so long an absence.
9. His faithful dog, Argus, was lying, old and decrepit, at the gate.
10. Argus started as Ulysses approached, knew him instantly, limped toward him, wagging his tail with joy, and then fell dead at his feet.

II. Grace Darling.

1. A steamship was wrecked on the coast amid a frightful storm.
2. Mr. Darling, the keeper of the light-house, saw the people clinging to the wreck and to the rocks.
3. He was afraid to venture out in his boat to rescue them.
4. His daughter Grace, a young woman, urged him to go, and let her accompany him.
5. They went, and, after dreadful dangers and difficulties, succeeded in saving nine of the people from a watery grave.
6. This conduct of Grace Darling gained for her very great praise and admiration.

[These exercises can be continued at the pleasure of the teacher. The sentences may be used for additional practice in analysis and parsing.]

LESSON CV.
DESCRIPTIVE COMPOSITIONS.

The pupil is here required to write a description of the object given, including the characteristics mentioned. He thus constructs sentences, and connects them.

EXAMPLE.—**The Whale.**

Points or Topics.—A very large animal. Sometimes called a fish. Not a fish. Warm-blooded. Breathes by means of lungs. A fish breathes through its gills. The whale must come to the surface to breathe, or *spout*. Has two fins (*flippers*), one on each side, and a flat, powerful tail. With this it can swim with great rapidity.

COMPOSITION.

The whale is a very large animal, sometimes called a fish; but it is not a fish, for it is warm-blooded, and breathes not by gills, like a fish, but by means of lungs. Therefore it must come to the surface to breathe, or *spout*. It has two fins (*flippers*), one on each side, and a flat, powerful tail, with which it can swim with great rapidity.

[The pupil should study this example very carefully, copying the composition in connection with the points or topics, then writing it once or twice, from the topics, so as to become familiar with the mode of constructing the sentences.]

Exercises.

In a similar manner, write compositions from the following, constructing sentences, and properly uniting them.

1. **The Reindeer.**—A very useful animal to the inhabitants of the Arctic regions. Of large size. Domesticated and made to do useful work. Not very graceful in shape. Tail very short. Little or no mane. Long shaggy hair on the front of the neck. Large branching horns. Flesh and milk excellent. Skin used by the Laplanders for various purposes. Can travel very fast and draw heavy loads.

2. **The Swan.**—A large swimming or water bird. Web-footed, like the goose and duck. Neck long and gracefully curving. Wings long and powerful. Flight high and rapid. Eyes

small and near the bill. Glides very gracefully over the water. Lives on grass, roots, and seeds, also on worms, insects, and small fishes. Plumage generally white.

3. **The Beaver.**—A valuable fur-bearing animal. Belongs to the order of quadrupeds called *rodents*, or gnawing animals. Body short and broad, from three to four feet long. Has a broad and flat tail. Uses this in building its dam and lodge. It carries the material for this between its chin and fore-paws. Places it with its fore-feet, patting it with its flat tail. An amphibious animal, so called because it lives on the land or in the water.

LESSON CVI.

LETTER-WRITING.

A letter consists of five parts ; namely, the **heading,** the **address,** the **body,** the **closing,** and the **superscription** (on the envelope).

The **heading** consists of the name of the place at which the letter is written, and the date.

This should be written a line or two from the top of the page, and should be commenced so that it may end near the margin of the sheet at the right. Thus :—

NEW YORK, July 10, 1889.

Or, when the street is mentioned :—

56 LAFAYETTE PLACE,
NEW YORK, July 10, 1889.

The **address** includes the name of the person to whom the letter is to be sent, and under this the proper term, or terms, of address ; as, *Sir* or *Madam*, *Dear Sir* or *Dear Madam*, etc.

The **body** of the letter is its chief part, containing what is designed to be said to the person to whom the letter is sent.

The **closing** is the formal expression of respect, compliment, or endearment which precedes the signature.

LETTER-WRITING.

The **superscription** is the statement, on the envelope, of the name and address of the person to whom the letter is to be sent.

Write the name about midway between the top and bottom of the envelope. Under this write the address, commencing each line a little farther to the right than that above it. Affix the postage-stamp to the right-hand corner at the top of the envelope.

The top of the envelope is that part which is turned down and lapped over in sealing.

Examples are here given.

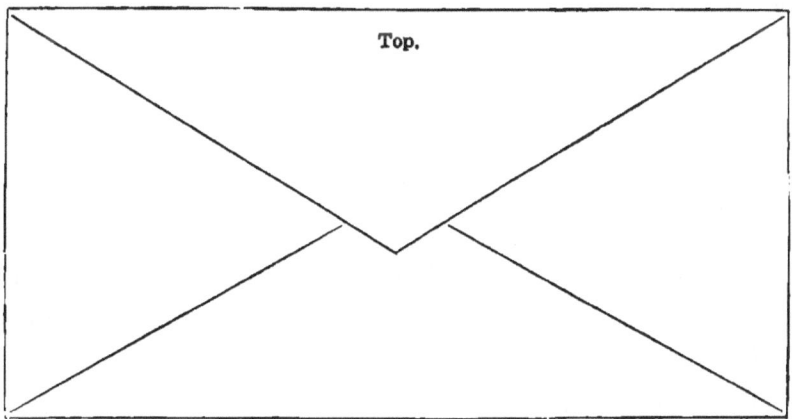

ENVELOPE SEALED.

Top.

ENVELOPE ADDRESSED.

Stamp.

Mr. Charles Johnson,
350 East Twelfth Street,
New York.

Exercise.

Write the following addresses upon blank envelopes, or blank pieces of paper cut into the form and shape of envelopes.

1. Mrs. William W. Hart, Milford, Pike Co., Pa.
2. Henry B. Cook, Esq., Cincinnati, O.
3. Mr. Thomas Brown, Baltimore, Md.
4. Miss Sophia H. Jones, 209 Tremont Street, Boston, Mass.
5. Messrs. William Wood & Company, 56 and 58 Lafayette Place, New York.
6. His Excellency D. B. Hill, Executive Chamber, Albany, N. Y.
7. Hon. S. S. Cox, M. C., House of Representatives, Washington, D. C.

LESSON CVII.

LETTER-WRITING.—FORMS OF ADDRESS.

The **address** should follow the *heading* on the line below, near the left side of the page, usually a little to the right of the body of the letter.

The following are examples.

1. For very formal letters :—

Mr. Thomas H. Brown,
  Springfield, Ill.
 Sir,

Mrs. T. H. Brown,
  Brooklyn, N. Y.
 Madam,

2. Ordinary style :—

Mr. William A. Thompson,
 Dear Sir, or
 My dear Sir,

Mrs. E. A. Jones,
 Dear Madam, or
 My dear Madam,

3. Implying greater intimacy :—

Dear Mr. Brown, or
My dear Mr. Brown,

Dear Miss Knox, or
My dear Mrs. James,

Other forms of address will be required according to circum-

LETTER-WRITING.—BODY AND CLOSING. 163

stances, varying with the persons addressed and the terms of intimacy that exist. Thus :—

A. B. Palmer, Esq.; John Porter, M.D.; Dr. John Porter; B. C. Baldwin, LL.D.; Rev. H. J. Davis, or Rev. Mr. Davis; or Rev. Noah Porter, D.D., LL.D.; etc.

In less formal letters the address may be written below and at the left of the signature, at the end of the letter.

The title *Hon.* is applied to persons holding high governmental positions; *His Excellency* is often applied to the President of the United States and to State Governors.

Exercise.

Write, one under the other, on a letter sheet, in the proper form, the following dates and addresses.

1. New York, May 10, 1889. Mr. Thomas Smith. Dear Sir,
2. Boston, June 1, 1889. Mr. William Porter. My dear Sir,
3. Philadelphia, January 5, 1889. Mrs. C. H. Smith. Dear Madam,
4. Cincinnati, March 15, 1889. Miss Thompson. Dear Madam,
5. Baltimore, April 2, 1889. A. B. Palmer, Esq. My dear Sir,
6. Savannah, July 1, 1889. My dear Friend,
7. Chicago, June 25, 1889. My dear Mr. Smith,
8. New York, August 5, 1889. The Rev. John Brown, D.D. Sir, *or*, Rev. and dear Sir,
9. Washington, D. C., September 1, 1889. Col. Henry Johnson, U. S. A. Dear Colonel,
10. Albany, N. Y., November 9, 1889. Hon. Levi P. Morton, Vice-President of the United States. Sir,

LESSON CVIII.
LETTER-WRITING.—BODY AND CLOSING.

The **body of the letter** should commence on the line next below the address, and a little to the right of it.

The style will, of course, vary with the character of the letter.

Business letters should be formal, brief, and to the point. Friendly correspondence requires an easy, familiar style.

A few specimens for the *opening* are here given:—

Yours of the 5th inst. is just received, etc.
Your favor of the 3d inst. is received, etc.
Your esteemed favor of the 10th inst. is at hand, etc.
I am in receipt of yours, etc.
Yours of the 20th ult. has remained unanswered until now, etc.

Closing.

The forms of closing, followed by the signature, are various. A few are here given:—

Respectfully yours; Very respectfully yours; Truly yours; Yours truly: Very truly yours: Your obedient servant: Your obedient, humble servant; Yours cordially; Faithfully yours; Yours affectionately; Ever affectionately yours; As ever, your friend; etc.

Specimen of a Business Letter.

New York, June 5, 1889.

Mr. John A. Jones.

Sir,

Your esteemed favor of the 19th inst. is just received. We shall forward to you without delay the mdse. which you order. Terms: three months credit, or 5 % discount for cash.

Respectfully yours,
William Brown & Co.

APPENDIX.

List of the Irregular Verbs.

These lists are to be referred to by the pupils as may be needed in preparing the exercises.

Present.	Preterit.	Imperf. Part.	Perfect Participle.
Abide,	abode,	abiding,	abode.
Arise,	arose,	arising,	arisen.
Be,	was,	being,	been.
Bear,	bore *or* bare,	bearing,	borne *or* born.*
Beat,	beat,	beating,	beat *or* beaten.
Begin,	began,	beginning,	begun.
Behold,	beheld,	beholding,	beheld.
Beseech,	besought,	beseeching,	besought.
Beset,	beset,	besetting,	beset.
Bid,	bid *or* băde,	bidding,	bid *or* bidden.
Bide,	bode,	biding,	bode.
Bind,	bound,	binding,	bound.
Bite,	bit,	biting,	bitten *or* bit.
Bleed,	bled,	bleeding,	bled.
Blow,	blew,	blowing,	blown.
Break,	broke,	breaking,	broken.
Breed,	bred,	breeding,	bred.
Bring,	brought,	bringing,	brought.
Burst,	burst,	bursting,	burst.
Buy,	bought,	buying,	bought.
Cast,	cast,	casting,	cast.
Chide,	chid,	chiding,	chidden *or* chid.
Choose,	chose,	choosing,	chosen.
Cleave,†	cleft *or* clove,	cleaving,	cleft *or* cloven.

---

* *Borne* signifies *carried;* *born* signifies *brought forth*.

† *Cleave,* to *split,* is irregular, as above; *cleave,* to *stick,* is regular, but *clave* was formerly used, in the preterit, for *cleaved.*

APPENDIX.

Present.	*Preterit.*	*Imperf. Part.*	*Perfect Participle.*
Cling,	clung,	clinging,	clung.
Come,	came,	coming,	come.
Cost,	cost,	costing,	cost.
Creep,	crept,	creeping,	crept.
Cut,	cut,	cutting,	cut.
Deal,	dealt,	dealing,	dealt.
Do,	did,	doing,	done.
Draw,	drew,	drawing,	drawn.
Drink,	drank,	drinking,	drunk *or* drank.
Drive,	drove,	driving,	driven.
Eat,	eat *or* ate,	eating,	eaten.
Fall,	fell,	falling,	fallen.
Feed,	fed,	feeding,	fed.
Feel,	felt,	feeling,	felt.
Fight,	fought,	fighting,	fought.
Find,	found,	finding,	found.
Flee,	fled,	fleeing,	fled.
Fling,	flung,	flinging,	flung.
Freeze,	froze,	freezing,	frozen.
Fly,	flew,	flying,	flown.
Forbear,	forbore,	forbearing,	forborne.
Forsake,	forsook,	forsaking,	forsaken.
Get,	got,	getting,	got *or* gotten.
Give,	gave,	giving,	given.
Go,	went,	going,	gone.
Grind,	ground,	grinding,	ground.
Grow,	grew,	growing,	grown.
Have,	had,	having,	had.
Hear,	heard,	hearing,	heard.
Hide,	hid,	hiding,	hidden *or* hid.
Hit,	hit,	hitting,	hit.
Hold,	held,	holding,	held *or* holden.
Hurt,	hurt,	hurting,	hurt.
Keep,	kept,	keeping,	kept.
Know,	knew,	knowing,	known.
Lay,	laid,	laying,	laid.
Lead,	led,	leading,	led.

APPENDIX. 167

Present.	Preterit.	Imperf. Part.	Perfect Participle.
Leave,	left,	leaving,	left.
Lend,	lent,	lending,	lent.
Let,	let,	letting,	let.
Lie (*to rest*),	lay,	lying,	lain.
Lose,	lost,	losing,	lost.
Make,	made,	making,	made.
Mean,	meant,	meaning,	meant.
Meet,	met,	meeting,	met.
Outdo,	outdid,	outdoing,	outdone.
Pay,	paid,	paying,	paid.
Put,	put,	putting,	put.
Read,	rĕad,	reading,	rĕad.
Rend,	rent,	rending,	rent.
Rid,	rid,	ridding,	rid.
Ride,	rode,	riding,	ridden.
Ring,	rang *or* rung,	ringing,	rung.
Rise,	rose,	rising,	risen.
Run,	ran *or* run,	running,	run.
Say,	said,	saying,	said.
See,	saw,	seeing,	seen.
Seek,	sought,	seeking,	sought.
Sell,	sold,	selling,	sold.
Send,	sent,	sending,	sent.
Set,	set,	setting,	set.
Shake,	shook,	shaking,	shaken.
Shed,	shed,	shedding,	shed.
Shoe,	shod,	shoeing,	shod.
Shoot,	shot,	shooting,	shot.
Shut,	shut,	shutting,	shut.
Shred,	shred,	shredding,	shred.
Shrink,	shrunk *or* shrank,	shrinking,	shrunk *or* shrunken.
Sing,	sung *or* sang,	singing,	sung.
Sink,	sunk *or* sank,	sinking,	sunk.
Sit,	sat,	sitting,	sat.
Slay,	slew,	slaying,	slain.
Sleep,	slept,	sleeping,	slept.
Slide,	slid,	sliding,	slid *or* slidden.

Present.	Preterit.	Imperf. Part.	Perfect Participle.
Sling,	slung,	slinging,	slung.
Slink,	slunk,	slinking,	slunk.
Smite,	smote,	smiting,	smitten *or* smit.
Speak,	spoke,	speaking,	spoken.
Spend,	spent,	spending,	spent.
Spin,	spun,	spinning,	spun.
Spit,	spit,	spitting,	spit.
Spread,	spread,	spreading,	spread.
Spring,	sprung *or* sprang,	springing,	sprung.
Stand,	stood,	standing,	stood.
Steal,	stole,	stealing,	stolen.
Stick,	stuck,	sticking,	stuck.
Sting,	stung,	stinging,	stung.
Stride,	strode,	striding,	stridden *or* strid.
Strike,	struck,	striking,	struck *or* stricken.
Strive,	strove,	striving,	striven.
Sweep,	swept,	sweeping,	swept.
Swear,	swore,	swearing,	sworn.
Swim,	swam,	swimming,	swum.
Swing,	swung,	swinging,	swung.
Take,	took,	taking,	taken.
Teach,	taught,	teaching,	taught.
Tear,	tore,	tearing,	torn.
Tell,	told,	telling,	told.
Think,	thought,	thinking,	thought.
Throw,	threw,	throwing,	thrown.
Thrust,	thrust,	thrusting,	thrust.
Tread,	trod,	treading,	trodden *or* trod.
Wear,	wore,	wearing,	worn.
Weave,	wove,	weaving,	woven.
Weep,	wept,	weeping,	wept.
Win,	won,	winning,	won.
Wind,	wound,	winding,	wound.
Wring,	wrung,	wringing,	wrung.
Write,	wrote,	writing,	written.

List of the Redundant Verbs.

Present.	Preterit.	Imperf. Part.	Perfect Participle.
Awake,	awoke or awaked,	awaking,	awaked.
Belay,	belaid or belayed,	belaying,	belaid or belayed.
Bend,	bent or bended,	bending,	bent or bended.
Bereave,	bereft or bereaved,	bereaving,	bereft or bereaved.
Bet,	bet or betted,	betting,	bet or betted.
Blend,	blended or blent,	blending,	blended or blent.
Bless,	blessed or blest,	blessing,	blessed or blest.
Build,	built or builded,	building,	built or builded.
Burn,	burned or burnt,	burning,	burned or burnt.
Catch,	caught or catched,	catching,	caught or catched.
Clothe,	clothed or clad,	clothing,	clothed or clad.
Crow,	crew or crowed,	crowing,	crowed.
Curse,	cursed or curst,	cursing,	cursed or curst.
Dare,	dared or durst,	daring,	dared.
Dig,	dug or digged,	digging,	dug or digged.
Dream,	dreamed or drĕamt,	dreaming,	dreamed or drĕamt.
Dress,	dressed or drest,	dressing,	dressed or drest.
Dwell,	dwelt or dwelled,	dwelling,	dwelt or dwelled.
Geld,	gelded or gelt,	gelding,	gelded or gelt.
Gild,	gilded or gilt,	gilding,	gilded or gilt.
Gird,	girded or girt,	girding,	girded or girt.
Grave,	graved,	graving,	graven or graved.
Hang,	hanged or hung,	hanging,	hanged or hung.
Heave,	heaved or hove,	heaving,	heaved or hoven.
Hew,	hewed,	hewing,	hewed or hewn.
Kneel,	knelt or kneeled,	kneeling,	knelt or kneeled.
Knit,	knit or knitted,	knitting,	knit or knitted.
Lade,	laded,	lading,	laded or laden.
Lean,	leaned or lĕant,	leaning,	leaned or lĕant.
Leap,	leaped or lĕapt,	leaping,	leaped or lĕapt.
Learn,	learned or learnt,	learning,	learned or learnt.
Light,	lighted or lit,	lighting,	lighted or lit.
Mow,	mowed,	mowing,	mowed or mown.
Pen (*to coop*),	penned or pent,	penning,	penned or pent.

APPENDIX.

Present.	Preterit.	Imperf. Part.	Perfect Participle.
Quit,	quitted *or* quit,	quitting,	quitted *or* quit.
Rap,	rapped,	rapping,	rapped *or* rapt.
Reave,	reft *or* reaved,	reaving,	reft *or* reaved.
Rive,	rived,	riving,	riven *or* rived.
Saw,	sawed,	sawing,	sawed *or* sawn.
Seethe,	seethed *or* sod,	seething,	seethed *or* sodden.
Shape,	shaped,	shaping,	shaped *or* shapen.
Shave,	shaved,	shaving,	shaved *or* shaven.
Shear,	sheared,	shearing,	sheared *or* shorn.
Shine,	shone *or* shined,	shining,	shone *or* shined.
Show,	showed,	showing,	shown *or* showed.
Slit,	slit *or* slitted,	slitting,	slit *or* slitted.
Smell,	smelled *or* smelt,	smelling,	smelled *or* smelt.
Sow,	sowed,	sowing,	sown *or* sowed.
Speed,	sped *or* speeded,	speeding,	sped *or* speeded.
Spell,	spelled *or* spelt,	spelling,	spelled *or* spelt.
Spill,	spilled *or* spilt,	spilling,	spilled *or* spilt.
Split,	split *or* splitted,	splitting,	split *or* splitted.
Spoil,	spoiled *or* spoilt,	spoiling,	spoiled *or* spoilt.
Stave,	staved *or* stove,	staving,	staved *or* stove.
Stay,	staid *or* stayed,	staying,	staid *or* stayed.
String,	strung,	stringing,	strung *or* stringed.
Strow,	strowed,	strowing,	strowed *or* strown.
Sweat,	sweat *or* sweated,	sweating,	sweat *or* sweated.
Swell,	swelled,	swelling,	swelled *or* swollen.
Thrive,	thrived,	thriving,	thriven *or* thrived.
Wax,	waxed,	waxing,	waxed *or* waxen.
Wet,	wet *or* wetted,	wetting,	wet *or* wetted.
Wont,	wont,	wonting,	wont *or* wonted.
Work,	worked *or* wrought,	working,	worked *or* wrought.

www.ingramcontent.com/pod-product-compliance
Lightning Source LLC
Chambersburg PA
CBHW031452160426
43195CB00010BB/942